Go For The Eagle

A Guide to Achieving
Scouting's Highest Rank

An easy-to-use Handbook for
Scouts, Leaders and Parents

By NANCY & DEAN HOCH

Foreword by Senator Orrin G. Hatch
Illustrations by Mike Beus
Photos By Barry Nelsen & Others

Copyright © 1987 by
Horizon Publishers & Distributors, Inc.

ISBN: 0-88290-359-4
Library of Congress No.: 87-080152
Horizon Publishers Catalog & Order No.: 2017
Third Printing, Revised   January 1990

Printed and distributed
in the United States of America by

Horizon
Publishers
& Distributors, Incorporated
P.O. Box 490 Bountiful, Utah 84011-0490

Dedicated to our five energetic Eagles and everyone who helped them reach their goal.

Acknowledgments

Scores of people contributed to the preparation of this book, and their assistance is deeply appreciated. The authors would especially like to acknowledge the following people for their assistance in reading the original drafts, for generously giving their insightful comments and suggestions or offering other special help: U. S. Senator Orrin G. Hatch, Jane and Barry Nelsen, Marilyn and John Johnson, Mary Croney, Jack and Deda Hilbert, Nancy Speer, Wayne Holiday, Ron Kloepfer, Bud Gardner, Phyllis Davidson, Jolene and David Anderson, Paul Jones, Glen Houghton and Darin Underwood.

Space does not allow the listing of all the other sources consulted in the preparation of this manual. These would include libraries, community institutions, newspaper offices and many individuals.

The authors express their heartfelt thanks to the staff at Horizon Publishers and all those who contributed to the preparation of this book.

Foreword

Almost without exception, every one of the thousands of boys who enter the Boy Scouts of America each year yearns for Scouting's highest award, the coveted Eagle rank. Each boy sets his sights on this honor, as do his parents and leaders. But only a small percentage of young men ever achieve it—less than two out of every hundred boys who enter the program become Eagles.

Part of the reason for this high dropout rate is that information on achieving the Eagle rank is lacking. Yet the need is certainly there. The benefits of the Eagle program both to the Scout and society cannot be calculated.

The rank speaks for itself. When a hundred boys apply for a job, the candidate who can write "EAGLE SCOUT" on his application has a much better chance of being hired. He's a young man recognized to have significant training and skills. He's an acknowledged leader.

Why do so many Scouts attain the first few ranks but never reach the highest? Nancy and Dean Hoch, the parents of five Eagle Scouts who served as Scouting leaders for over 15 years, can tell you why. They do just that in this timely book and also offer dozens of simple guidelines to achieving the rank. In a few brief chapters, they outline a step-by-step guide to Scouting's most outstanding achievement.

The authors have been involved in Scouting for many years, both as parents and as leaders. Nancy Hoch worked in the area of Scouting Advancement. Dean Hoch was in Scouting in his youth and has also served as Scoutmaster and committee member. He has seen the benefits of Scouting in his work as an educator in the public schools. As the father of five Eagles, he's been on more campouts and Scouting activities than he might care to count.

Besides their other activities, they have written articles for many national magazines including *Good Housekeeping; Venture: The Magazine for Entrepreneurs; The Runner; National Gardening Magazine; Mother Earth News; Success Magazine;* and others. They have also written a book on *Continuing Education for the Professions.*

Editorial Assistant Barry Nelsen is a photo-journalist who has written articles on the Scouting program. He has served as a leader in the Scouting organization, spending much time in out-of-doors activities with Scouts and on the trail. He has also spearheaded successful fundraising endeavors and has been involved in Scouting service projects.

Much of the material supplied in this manual cannot be found elsewhere. It is information gleaned from first-hand experience. Because of it, the road to Eagle will be more effectively walked by a greater number of young men.

As long as there are boys working toward the Eagle rank, leaders hoping to guide them successfully, and parents who want to give their sons effective support, this book will be of great value.

Orrin G. Hatch
United States Senate
Washington, D. C.

Contents

Did you know?
Famous Eagles
Why only a small percentage of Scouts ever reach Eagle rank
The naming of a world famous rank
What are the rewards?
One additional benefit

(The Program At A Glance)

Introducing Scotty Scout
The basic trail - step by step
Making use of the *Boy Scout Handbook*
Cub Scouting: An important foundation
Starting up the Scouting trail
A simple, easy-to-use record form
How far, how fast?
Completing the basic requirements
Scotty becomes a Star
The basics of merit badge work
Leadership requirements
Service hours
Last step before Eagle: Life rank
The Eagle is within reach

*(The Importance Of A Motivated Scout, A
Good Leader, And A Willing Family Member)*

The boy - the goal
A special note to Scouts
The important leadership support
A special note to leaders
The family - the goal

A special note to parents
A note to both leaders and parents

Why service hours?
It's easy as one, two, three
Keeping a record of service hours
A list of service project ideas

What's required?
The fabulous "Fifty-miler"
Don't forget Scout camp
Attention: Scoutmasters
Keep a record of all overnighters
Limitless activities

Keep a calendar
Sample Eagle project calendar
Selecting a project
Projects that *do not* qualify
Getting approval
Onward into the project
The big day arrives
The finishing touches
Something to think about

Do it while it's fresh
Seven easy steps
Do a draft first, then do the final copy
Sketches and photos
Project write-up checklist
Sample project write-up
Sample Eagle project photos

Making it all a little easier
Letters of recommendation

Charts, Lists and Checklists, Illustrations, Photos, and Sample Documents

Why This Book Was Written

Our oldest son nearly missed attaining the Eagle rank. This was because we, as parents, did not understand what we needed to know about the steps involved. Luckily, he was not one of the many boys who "falls through the cracks." As he and our other boys went through the program, we learned why so many boys never reach their goal.

Any boy going for Scouting's highest rank will find the "nuts and bolts" of the program in his *Official Boy Scout Handbook*. This is an excellent reference source for Scouting skills and various merit badge material. However, our experience has shown that much more information is needed for boys who are serious about earning the Eagle rank. This book, *Go For The Eagle!*, is not meant to take away from the official literature of the Boy Scouts of America but rather to compliment it.

As many who have worked in Scouting know, there are aspects of the Eagle program that are somewhat "fuzzy" and undefined. For example, very little is spelled out as to how a boy handles all the details for his Eagle project. And there are few helps given to him for his project write-up. We have never read about the use of separate file folders for each merit badge a boy attempts or how a Scout can best keep track of his service hours or campouts. Little information is available that tells parents and leaders the steps in planning a memorable Eagle Court of Honor.

It even took some research for us to dig out the many reasons *why* the Eagle is such a valuable goal to work toward. And these are just a few of the areas needing more explanation if more boys are ever going to go for the Eagle and get it. That's what this book is all about.

During the years our sons went through the ranks, we learned that many Scout leaders and parents struggle with these same problem areas in the Eagle program. We could see that the gaps in the needed information were preventing boys from fully experiencing the benefits of the Scout advancement program. Boys simply were dropping out because of the reasons listed in this book— reasons that *can* be overcome.

Go For The Eagle offers new and helpful information. It provides useful guidelines and presents valuable checklists at the end of several chapters. This is information not found elsewhere.

Scotty Scout, the illustrated character who frequently appears in this book, will serve as your guide. He will lead you all the way from Cub Scout days to the coveted rank.

Our goal in writing this book is to smooth the way, provide helpful hints, and make the Eagle rank a reality for more young men.

Nancy & Dean Hoch

1
Why The Eagle?

Did You Know?

That Scouting's alumni includes. . .
   63% of Air Force Academy graduates
   68% of West Point graduates
   70% of Annapolis graduates
   72% of Rhodes scholars
   85% of F.B.I. agents
   26 of the first 29 astronauts
   85% of student council presidents
   89% of senior class presidents

Did You Know?

That for every 100 youth that join Scouting. . .
  12 will have their first contact with a church
  5 will earn their church's religious emblem
  1 will enter the clergy
  18 will develop hobbies that will last through their adult life
  8 will enter a career that was introduced through the merit badge system
  1 will use Scouting skills to save another person's life
  1 will use Scouting skills to save his own life
  17 will become Scouting volunteers
  2 will become Eagle Scouts

These figures, published in a Northern California's Golden Empire Council Newsletter, are from a survey of Scouts and non-Scouts in various schools and colleges around the country.

Just looking at these numbers gives some good reasons for a boy to become a Scout. If only Eagles had been studied, these figures would be even more remarkable.

When a boy climbs the ladder to Eagle, he'll develop skills and character traits that will benefit him all his life. These include:

  Leadership
  Perseverance
  The quality of living up to high principles
  The ability to work with others
  Self-reliance
  Initiative
  Endurance
  Communications abilities
  Employment orientation in many fields
  All the basic Scouting skills
  And much more!

Looking at the lives and accomplishments of Eagle Scouts helps us appreciate this distinguished award even more.

Famous Eagles

Steven Spielberg, one of the most successful movie directors of all time, became an Eagle Scout at age 13. As a very young boy, he enrolled in a Boy Scout photography program. That program was the first step that led him all the way to the highest rank in Scouting. It also helped him go to the top in his chosen career.

Spielberg jokingly said in a May 31, 1982 *Time Magazine* article, "If I hadn't been a Scout, I'd probably have ended up as an ax murderer or a butcher in a Jewish deli."

And that, of course, is the whole point! The Scouting program, and particularly the Eagle Scout advancement program, gives a young man a completely new orientation in the way he thinks—about himself, about others and about his future. It can take him all the way to the top in whatever he's trying to achieve—to the top and even beyond. How high? How about as high as the moon?

When Eagle Scout Neil Armstrong landed on the moon and took that "one giant step for mankind," he had gone higher than any human being had ever gone before. And we can assume it is no small coincidence that this famous mark in history was made by a boy who had gone as high as he could in his Scouting career as well. He was a "go-getter." He set the goal of Eagle and achieved that goal at an early age. He also set a pattern that would see him through all the other goal-setting experiences of his life.

That's why the Eagle!

Captain James Lovell piloted the Apollo 13 space flight through its dangerous emergency return to Earth. He also circled the moon in Apollo 8's mission during the 1968 Christmas season. Lovell, too, is an Eagle Scout and proud of it. Lovell praises Scouting for the lessons it taught him. "I owe much of my present career to the training I received as a Boy Scout," he says. "It was through Scouting that I first learned self-reliance, leadership, and many of the other fine attributes Scouting has to offer."

Other famous Eagles include former United States President Gerald Ford, NBC Newscaster Frank Blair, Associate Justice of the Supreme Court Thomas C. Clark, Major General Lawrence Snowden of the U.S. Marine Corps, General William Westmoreland of the U.S. Army and Admiral Elmo Russell Zumwalt, Jr. of the U.S. Navy—just to name a few of the many thousands of famous Eagle Scouts. The list goes on and on.

Why Only a Small Percentage
of Scouts Ever Reach Eagle Rank

The two biggest reasons boys drop out of the Scouting program before achieving its highest rank are:

  1) lack of motivation
  2) lack of support.

The Scout going for Eagle has to be highly interested in the
program. And he needs the support of a good Scout leader.
It's also a great help to have a family member who cares about
his advancement. This threesome (the boy, the leader, and an
interested family member) is discussed more in Chapter 3. It's
a "three-legged" stool concept and an important key to success in the Eagle program.

Other reasons for a Scout's failure to reach Eagle might be:
  • A lack of consistent effort.
  • Waiting too long between rank advancements.
  • Not getting most of the work done before high school
    age when too many other interests begin to compete.
  • Being afraid to tackle the Eagle Scout service project.
  • Getting bogged down in all the paperwork.
  • Lack of proper advancement records being kept.

Each of these difficulties can be overcome. It's important,
however, to know where the danger zones are and how to overcome them. The solutions to all the above problems are covered in the following chapters.

The Naming of a World Famous Rank

Did you know the Eagle rank was originally called the Wolf
rank? It was the popular American naturalist-illustrator-author,
Ernest Thompson Seton, who first introduced the idea of awards
for Scouting achievement. He relayed some of his "Red Indian
Boy Scouts of America" ideas to England's General Robert S.
S. Baden-Powell.

Baden-Powell quickly caught the idea. In his book, *Scouting
For Boys,* published back in 1908, he introduced badges deal-

ing with specific subjects. For outstanding achievement he added an extra special badge called the "The Wolf" badge.

Later, in the United States, the question kept being asked, "Why Wolf as the designation of Scouting's highest rank? Why not the American Eagle?" The requests were so persistent that in 1912 the change was finally made.

Some Scouters may not be aware that the founders of our nation once wanted the turkey as our national bird. Benjamin Franklin was one who fought long and hard to give the turkey this distinction.

The very first recipient of the Eagle badge was Arthur R. Eldred of Troop 1, Rockville Center, New York. Everyone wanted to be sure this first Eagle Scout was qualified to receive his award. So he was reviewed not only by his own troop's board of review but also by the nation's three major Scouting figures. Today it would be like having the three highest Scout executives from the National Scout Office as a review board.

Eldred's presentation was a grand affair, with many of Scouting's original founders in attendance. It set the stage for all the Eagle presentations to follow. There were to be over a million such Eagle awards given in the next 75 years.

Any Scout who joins this illustrious group of Eagles can be proud. He has accomplished something remarkable in his young life.

What Are The Rewards?

A Scout not only learns important skills and develops excellent character traits on the trail to Eagle. He can also expect some very tangible rewards as well.

When he submits an application for a scholarship or for a job, he should include information on earning the Eagle award. This will almost always give him a significant advantage over the other applicants.

Just as the fledgling bird looks up to the adult Eagle, so the Tenderfoot Scout dreams of one day achieving Eagle rank.

More and more Rhodes Scholarships are being awarded to Eagle Scouts. Businesses and professions seek them—so do governmental organizations. The opportunities are almost endless for the young man who starts out as a struggling baby eagle (a Tenderfoot Scout) who grows, develops and soars to the heights of the Scouting program.

One Additional Benefit

A big part of the early days of a Scout's career involves knot tying. Some boys love it. Others find it a nagging challenge. All must learn the many kinds of knots that serve important functions. Some, correctly tied, have even saved lives.

The young man who learns his knots well once again benefits throughout his life. However, it will be in a way he would probably never anticipate. As he progresses up the ladder to Eagle, he will constantly be reviewing his knots. One day he'll look back and realize he not only learned to tie the kinds of knots that require an actual rope. He'll also realize he learned to tie "knots" that will "hold securely" in his relationships in life. He'll be the man who can hang on through difficult times—the kind of man who won't come loose and fall apart under pressure. He will have learned to tie another important kind of knot—the kind that cannot be seen.

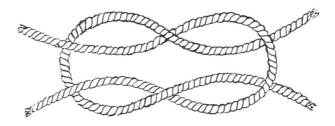

The Eagle Scout program has proven itself. So have the Eagles it has produced.

The challenge is to have more boys achieve the coveted rank and enjoy the benefits of the full program offered by the Boy Scouts of America. This book is meant to help make this goal a reality.

2

How Do You
Eat An Elephant?

(The Program
At A Glance)

In the middle of a conversation about Scouting you might hear someone say, "I made it to First Class." The reply may be, "I only got to Tenderfoot." A third fellow might sadly remark, "I missed Eagle by only two merit badges!"

To someone who doesn't know Scouting, these comments would have little meaning. To someone who does, they indicate the various levels of Scouting advancement. A knowledge of them is vital to a boy reaching Eagle rank.

It helps to be able to see the Eagle advancement program "at a glance," so to speak. That's what this chapter is all about. It also gives information not found elsewhere that will help a boy toward his goal.

The ranks of Scouting can be thought of as steps up the ladder to the organization's most outstanding achievement. To some boys and, unfortunately, even to some leaders, the ranks sometime seem like an impossible challenge. However, advancing through them is a necessary part of the Eagle program.

How do you eat an elephant? Scotty Scout wonders how he will EVER get all those merit badges, do his Eagle project and complete all the other requirements for Eagle.

Introducing Scotty Scout

First, let's meet Scotty Scout. He's Mr. Average Boy Scout, and we want to see how he progresses through those ranks.

Just how is Scotty going to get from the first step, Scout rank, all the way to Eagle? Well, how does someone eat an elephant (or a hamburger, for that matter)?

You're right. The answer, of course, is bite by bite.

If each boy, his leader and his parents see this as a step-by-step activity, the whole process becomes quite manageable. They will understand that Scotty Scout needs to accomplish certain goals within a certain period of time for him to achieve each rank advancement.

This will be a valuable experience for any young man, since much of life revolves around this same principle. The Scout advancement program allows a young man to receive recognition each step of the way. If a four-month "jump" from one rank to another takes a boy six months, that's okay. He doesn't race against the calendar. He races against his own timetable, and he can advance at his own pace.

But the *key* is not to linger too long within any one rank. Slow progress causes discouragement, and the Scout may begin to lose interest in the program. The more he moves along, receiving his rank patches and merit badges on a regular basis, the more incentive he'll have to continue.

The Basic Trail—Step By Step

Let's take a brief look at the Scouting advancement program. To see the big picture, study the *Suggested Time Line* at the end of this chapter. This chart shows some realistic goals for a boy going for Eagle rank. The projected schedule is explained in detail in the following paragraphs.

Making Use Of The Boy Scout Handbook

The *Official Boy Scout Handbook* may be purchased at any local Scout service center and at some department stores. It is Scotty Scout's major tool to help him advance up the Eagle trail. The actual advancement records are found in the back of the book. Scotty and his parents will need to refer to this section often. The Scout leader sees these pages frequently since he has to sign for each achievement.

The rest of the Handbook is devoted to providing basic Scouting data. It contains essential information on the requirements for Eagle.

The Handbook is also valuable as a day-to-day reference book. An FBI agent who was also a popular Scoutmaster once told his troop, "That Handbook is one of the most valuable books I own. I've carried mine with me for years. In FBI work, it's a great help. It gives me vital data in an illustrated, easy-to-use form. It really has become my number one home and general reference source for a lot of important information."

This is why Scouts who study their Handbooks can save lives. It's also why they become masters of many varied skills.

Cub Scouting: An Important Foundation

The Scout who goes through the Cub Scout program is fortunate. Starting at age 7, a boy learns some of the fundamentals of Scouting. Along with having fun, he sees what lies ahead as he earns his activity badges and progresses through the Cub ranks.

As a first grader he enters the Cub Scout program and becomes a Tiger Scout. In second grade, he's a Wolf Scout, and in third grade a Bear Scout. In the 4th and 5th grades he will be in the two-year Webelo program. Webelos stands for **We'll Be Loyal** Scouts.

Starting Up The Scouting Trail

A boy who has never been a Cub Scout can, of course, very successfully enter the Boy Scout program. The two programs are independent of each other as far as rank advancements and awards are concerned.

Any boy can officially become a Boy Scout when he completes the fifth grade, or is 11 years old, or has earned the Arrow of Light Award. From age 11 to age 14 the boy is part of a Boy Scout troop. At age 14 he becomes a Varsity Scout and at age 16 he enters an Explorer Post. Age 18 marks the end of the actual Boy Scout program.

To become an Eagle a young man must complete all his work and submit his papers *before* his eighteenth birthday. This is a hard and fast rule. There are few, if any, exceptions.

When a Scout first comes into the program, he earns his Scout rank patch by completing the requirements outlined in his handbook and by having a Scoutmaster conference.

He then progresses through Tenderfoot, Second Class, and First Class. No time requirements are set for these rank advancements.

A Simple, Easy-To-Use Record Form

Page 34 shows a one-page record of Scotty Scout's advancement toward Eagle. This is called his *Go For The Eagle Chart*. It combines information from several official and unofficial Scout forms. The big advantage of this form is that it offers a quick way of keeping track of Scotty's advancement. *It shows everything on one page.*

The *Go For The Eagle Chart* gives Scotty, his parents and leaders a bird's eye view of the trail to Eagle. It should be placed on the refrigerator or in another easy-to-see place where the family can readily check on their Scout's progress. This record should be used along with the advancement pages in the back of Scotty's *Official Boy Scout Handbook*.

This "Go for the Eagle" chart lets me see where I am at a glance.

Scoutmasters and advancement chairpeople will also find this one-page record a great tool for keeping track of each boy's advancement. These charts, when kept in alphabetical order, provide easy record-keeping for an entire troop of Scouts.

How Far—How Fast?

It's not wise for a boy to earn his Eagle too quickly. He needs time in Scouting to develop and grow. He needs to exercise leadership and develop maturity. On the other hand, he should not wait too long to earn the majority of his requirements. This is an aspect of the program that needs careful consideration by the Scout leader.

One 80-year-old Scoutmaster once said at a Court of Honor, "There's only one way to raise a boy—that's to bury him when he's 12 or 13 and dig him up again when he's 18 or 19." Then he added, "However, if we did that, we'd never have any Eagle Scouts!" It's that important time in the early teens when all the groundwork for the Eagle needs to be laid.

A often-adopted goal is for a young man to try to have his Eagle requirements completed before he enters high school. Of course, he has until he turns 18 to earn the rank. However, if he does not have his requirements nearly finished by the time

"Go For The Eagle" Chart

Scout's Name _____

Address _____

Phone _____

Birth Date _____

Date Registered as a Boy Scout _____

RANK ADVANCEMENT DATES

Scout Rank _____

Tenderfoot _____

Second Class _____

First Class _____

(GOAL-First Class by age 12)

Star _____

Life _____

(GOAL-Life by age 14)

Eagle _____

(GOAL-Eagle before high school)

Bronze Palm _____

Gold Palm _____

Silver Palm _____

SERVICE HOURS—DATE COMPLETED:

1 hour while 2nd Class _____

6 hours while Star _____

Eagle Project while Life _____

LEADERSHIP POSITIONS HELD AND DATES:

Six months while Star Scout:

POSITION _____

From _____ To _____

Six months while Life Scout:

POSITION _____

From _____ To _____

MERIT BADGE LIST (21 are required)

Must earn: **Date earned:**

First Aid _____

Citizenship in Community _____

Citizenship in Nation _____

Citizenship in World _____

Communications _____

Environmental Science _____

Personal Management _____

Safety _____

Emergency Preparedness *or* Lifesaving _____

Personal Fitness *or* Swimming *or* Sports _____

Camping _____

Elective Badges: Choose any 10 from *Boy Scout*
Requirements booklet:

1. _____

2. _____

3. _____

4. _____

5. _____

6. _____

7. _____

8. _____

9. _____

10. _____

he starts high school, he will be approaching the age when too many other interests will compete for his time and attention: girls, cars, sports, work and so forth.

So, shoot for the Eagle early.

Looking more closely at the *Suggested Time Line* shown at the end of this chapter, we see that Scotty should try for his First Class rank before he turns 12. He can work on his Tenderfoot, Second Class, and First Class requirements all at one time, if he chooses. He earns white beads for Tenderfoot requirements, green beads for Second Class requirements, and red beads for First Class requirements. These beads he displays on his leather belt loop.

All boards of review for rank advancements are held by the Scout Committee except for the Eagle Board of Review. This board of review will be discussed later in the book.

Completing The Basic Requirements

In addition to the work described so far, each rank advancement from Tenderfoot to First Class also requires the following:

Basic Rank Advancement Requirements

Active attendance and participation
Showing Scout Spirit
 (Living the Scout oath and law)
A Scoutmaster conference
 (a goal-setting meeting with the Scoutmaster)
A board of review

With First Class under his belt (actually all his beads are literally "on his belt" and his First Class patch is earned), Scotty Scout can look forward to three more levels: Star, Life and Eagle.

Right away he can see his goal is within reach. At this point, it doesn't look impossible at all.

However, this is the time to realize that the last three jumps will take some hard work and much independent effort on the part of every Scout going to the top.

Scotty Becomes A Star

Four months must pass after Scotty Scout earns First Class for him to qualify for the Star patch. During this time he has to earn five merit badges, including any three from the required list for Eagle. The eleven required badges are:

> *First Aid* (earned for First Class rank)
> *Citizenship in the Community*
> *Citizenship in the Nation*
> *Citizenship in the World*
> *Communications*
> *Environmental Science*
> *Personal Management*
> *Safety*
> *Emergency Preparedness*
>   or *Lifesaving*
> *Personal Fitness*
>   or *Swimming*
>   or *Sports*
> *Camping*

Some of these badges are earned with troop effort involved. Others may be earned at Scout camp. *Most are earned through individual effort.*

The Basics Of Merit Badge Work

As Scotty goes for each merit badge, here are the important steps he needs to take:

- Talk over plans for the merit badge with the Scoutmaster. Ask him to sign a merit badge card.
- Read the merit badge pamphlet for that particular badge to become more familiar with it.
- Ask the Scoutmaster for a list of approved counselors. Call the one who lives closest and make an appointment.
- Be on time for the appointment. Take along the merit badge card, a notebook, paper and pencil and any other materials that might be needed. Wear the Scout uniform, of course, and be neat and clean in appearance.

- Be attentive to the information the counselor offers. Take notes on what needs to be done. Be sure everything is clear. Set a time for the next appointment to save a phone call. Note the date and time on the note pad.
- *Then, begin the actual work on the merit badge. Call the counselor if anything is not clear.*
- When the work on the badge is complete, go for the second appointment. Be ready to pass off the badge or get more information, if that is needed. Merit badge counselors will be impressed if all materials are in a file folder or notebook and if it's obvious that some significant work has been done by the Scout.
- Be sure the merit badge card is ready to be signed if the badge is to be completed at this second appointment.
- If the work is passed off satisfactorily, the counselor will sign the merit badge card usually in *two* places. Note: Some cards have a tear-off section that the counselor keeps in his or her records.
- The card is then returned to the Scoutmaster for recording in troop records and should finally be given to the person in charge of advancement for the troop. Some councils use a card that has a tear off section that allows a boy to keep a record of the badge in his home files. If this is not the case, the boy should note in his merit badge file all the important information from the card. This would include the date, counselor's name and phone number.
- *It's important for the Scout to have a record of each badge he earns.* Once in a blue moon both the counselor and the people on the troop committee may misplace their information on the badge. The only verification that the merit badge work has been done may be the Scout's information. This kind of record keeping may save a Scout from having to repeat a badge.

Leadership Requirements

It's while going for Star rank that Scotty begins to really develop his leadership skills. He serves for six months in one or more of the following capacities:

Den Chief
Chaplain Aide
Librarian
Scribe
Instructor
Musician
Patrol Leader
Assistant Senior Patrol Leader
Senior Patrol Leader
Leadership Corps
Junior Assistant Scoutmaster

Each troop or council can provide more information on the leadership positions and what they require. Most assignments are picked by the Patrol Leader and his assistant—with the approval of the Scoutmaster. The positions of Senior Patrol Leader and Patrol Leader are assigned by the Scoutmaster.

The Scout needs to record the dates he serves in each leadership position. This is important to note in his handbook and also on his one-page *Go For The Eagle Chart.* This cannot be stressed enough since some Scouts advance through the program with everything in order except the verification of leadership time served.

If a boy is not given a leadership position, the parent should contact the troop leaders to find out when he will be given one.

Service Hours

For Star rank, Scotty also must offer service to his community. He is required to participate in *not less* than six hours of volunteer work of some kind. These service hours do not have to be done all at once, nor all on one project. (See Chapter 4, *Preparation for the Big One: Making Those Service Hours Meaningful*).

To complete Star rank, the Scout must again pass off the "basic requirements" listed previously for First Class.

Last Step Before Eagle: Life Rank

Now Scotty Scout knows what's expected of him. He repeats the pattern he set for Star rank by earning five more merit badges including three more from the required list. He serves in a leadership position, gives six more hours of service and once again meets the "basic requirements."

Another six months elapse, and he's a Life Scout if, of course, he has completed all the requirements. This again is where it's best not to let too much extra time pass between rank advancements. Six months is usually sufficient time to complete the Life rank requirements.

The Scout, his parents, the Scoutmaster, and the advancement person all need to be checking the *Go For The Eagle Chart.* They need to make sure goals are being met and that progress is going according to schedule.

The Eagle Is Within Reach

During the final six months of the program, Scotty has to push on and complete ten more merit badges. He finishes up the remainder of the required work and chooses elective badges out of the more than 100 listings in the *Boy Scout Requirements* booklet.

Again, he must serve in one of the leadership positions on a regular basis and complete "the basics."

His service to the community must take the form of the more advanced Eagle Scout Service Project. This will be reviewed in detail in Chapter 6.

With the completion of all the above—plus the details outlined in the chapters to follow—the Eagle Award will be in hand. And it will all have been accomplished as an elephant gets eaten, bite-by-bite—or as a mountain is climbed, step-by-step.

As mentioned earlier, this chapter gives an overview and some clarification of rank advancement requirements. Scouts should follow the *Official Boy Scout Handbook* for further guidelines.

Use the remainder of *this book* to assist with the other, less-defined areas of the Eagle program.

Go For The Eagle Suggested Time Line

Cub Scouts	First Year of Scouts	2nd & 3rd Year of Scouts	Varsity Scouts	Explorer Program
Ages 7-11	Ages 11-12	Ages 12-14	Ages 14-16	Ages 16 to 18
Try for Arrow of Light	Earn Scout rank Earn Tenderfoot Earn Second Class Earn First Class	Earn Star rank Earn Life rank	Earn Eagle rank	Continue in Post activities and scout leadership activities
Cubbing Days	*You're On Your Way*	*You're Getting Closer*	*You Made It!*	*Onward Ever Onward*
NOTE: *Not required for Eagle.*	NOTE: *Allow one year or less to complete.*	NOTE: *Can be done in ten months. Allow about 18 months to complete*	NOTE: *Can be done in six months. A Scout should shoot for earning all the Eagle requirements before entering high school.*	NOTE: *This age Scout makes a great camp counselor. He can be an excellent leader and an example to younger Scouts.*

SPECIAL NOTE: A Scout has until he turns 18 to complete all the requirements for Eagle. However, this time line is a practical and realistic way to set goals to assure earning the Eagle rank. *The suggested time frames are approximate.*

The Team Approach to Achieving Eagle Rank:
The "Three Legged Stool"
1. A motivated Scout
2. A dedicated leader
3. A well-informed parent.

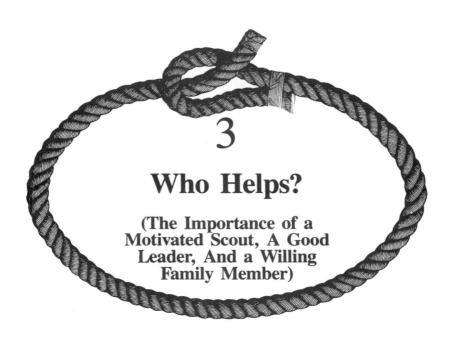

3

Who Helps?

(The Importance of a Motivated Scout, A Good Leader, And a Willing Family Member)

What's the magic formula? How does a Scout climb that challenging trail to Eagle rank? Alone, it would be very difficult. So where does he get the help he needs? In this chapter we will talk about that important support.

A big part of the process is much like a three-legged stool. It requires:

    (1) a strong, dedicated boy

    (2) an interested and enthusiastic Scout leader

    (3) almost always, an informed and devoted parent or family member.

Without all three being "on the ball," it's a rare boy who reaches Scouting's highest goal.

All three "legs of the stool" need to be familiar with the *Official Boy Scout Handbook*. They need to check the rank advancement information in the back of the handbook frequently. AND all three need to be looking at the one-page *Go For The Eagle Chart* on page 34.

This way the Scout, along with his parents and leaders, will be sure progress is being made at the appropriate times. They will know if Scotty's advancements are taking place when they should. Sometimes just a brief reminder is all he will need to keep him moving up the ladder.

It would also be a good idea for the Scoutmaster and the parents to check their records periodically with the committee member in charge of advancement. Then everything will be in agreement and officially recorded.

Any Scout not making progress on a regular basis is likely to quit trying. Parents and leaders can do a lot to prevent this from happening just by giving encouragement and showing interest along the way.

The Boy—The Goal

Most Scouts look to the Eagle rank as something wonderful. They know it's a possibility. They've seen other boys achieve it. Most look forward to the day when they will earn it themselves.

To get to Eagle rank, however, each Scout has to be *motivated.* He has to make a commitment to his goal. If he does this, he's on his way, and he'll find his family and his Scout leaders are going to be the biggest assets he has in helping him go all the way to the top.

A Special Note To Scouts

You, the Scout, are the "main man" in this whole effort. You will have help, of course, but *you must be the one who sets the goal and does the work.*

Part of your responsibilty is keeping good records of what you do. You need to set up a *Go For The Eagle* file folder. You will keep important papers in this folder. You also need to keep separate folders on *each* of your merit badges.

For example, when working on First Aid, have a file folder labeled "First Aid." Keep all the information on the First Aid merit badge in this folder. Have it with you when you work on the badge. Take it when you go to the counselor to have the badge signed off. Keep it on hand for reference. Much of the information also will be helpful for school reports.

Do the same for each of the 21 merit badges you must earn. These folders will allow you to have everything handy and in one place. They will save repeated effort and keep notes from being lost or misplaced. The folders will be an excellent record of what has been done along the trail to Eagle. Scouts who do not use this system often waste time with much duplicated effort.

Records must also be kept of camping and service hours. These will be described later in the book.

Just remember, the whole process takes place little by little, and it's all part of the experience of becoming an Eagle Scout.

That Important Leadership Support

A good Scoutmaster is *so* important! He can make or break a boy's interest in the whole Eagle program. He has to know the program and love it, and he needs to be aware of each boy's climb toward Eagle rank.

Besides the Scoutmaster, the local troop Scout Committee can be most helpful to the Eagle candidate. Good leadership from this group can inspire boys to go all the way to their goal. One family representative for each boy in the troop makes for an ideal Scout Committee. Other interested community members are always welcome.

The Scout Committee has many areas where people may serve. Some require a lot of time, some just a little. The support of this group to the Scoutmaster can be incalculable.

Committee meetings are usually held once a month for an hour. That's all that's needed to move the program along. A newsletter from the committee is helpful and informative for

Scouts and their families. (See a sample newsletter at the end of this chapter.)

Some committees have the boys submit designs for the troop's letterhead. One of the Scouts and his family may assume responsibility for the newsletter for a few months and then turn it over to another family. The time spent may qualify for service hours.

When each family receives a newsletter each month, there's no excuse for anyone missing meetings. Also, through a newsletter, boys in the troop receive extra recognition for their accomplishments.

Perhaps the single most important member of the Scout Committee is the person in charge of advancement. This person is called the Advancement Committee Member and must be an accurate record keeper. He or she submits troop advancement forms to the council service center on a regular basis. This way an official record is kept on each Scout.

Individual troops are responsible for keeping their own records. When news of advancement is transferred to council records, the advancement person uses the official advancement report form. One copy is kept in the troop files by date, and two copies go to the council office.

When the Eagle candidate submits his papers, these reports become vitally important. They verify each Scout's rank advancements and all the merit badges he has earned. If any questions arise, the Scout will need to have his own record of the work available. This information and the troop records will verify his work.

Besides keeping records, the person in charge of advancement acts as a catalyst for the troop by checking on each boy periodically. With just a simple reminder phone call now and then, the person in charge of advancement keeps a boy moving toward his goal.

A mother of three Eagle Scouts served as the local troop's committee member in charge of advancement for several years. She had this to say:

"When I first get involved in anything like this, I read everything I can get my hands on. I get an overall view of what can happen."

She adds, "To motivate boys, you need to avoid negative thoughts that might keep you from giving it all you've got."

This particular "go get'em" Advancement Committee Member has shepherded many young men along the trail to Eagle. She knows the program and puts much time and effort into helping boys toward their goal.

She adds, "Boys need to know you are truly concerned about them. They need constant follow-up and encouragement."

In a similar vein, psychologist Rudolph Dreikurs says: "A child needs encouragement as much as a plant needs water." This is particularly true as a boy progresses through his Scouting career.

A Special Note To Leaders

All Scouts in the troop should be receiving their beads, merit badges and rank advancements *as soon as possible* after they are earned.

It's important to have Courts of Honor frequently—at least every three months for an active troop of boys. These events are real motivators. They allow all the boys to see where the other boys are in relation to their own progress. They also allow public recognition of achievement and keep everyone's efforts going in the right direction.

The Family—The Goal

Many parents and family members assume the Scoutmaster will do all the work necessary to get their boy to Eagle rank. *W R O N G !* Remember, Scoutmasters are volunteer workers. They give of their time without monetary pay. A boy may have several of them during his climb to Eagle. Members of the committee also change assignments and go on to other things. Only the interested family member can provide the on-going support that's so important.

A word of caution, however. You may have heard about universities that give a special "degree" to wives who help put their husbands through their Ph.D. programs. The degree is called the Ph.T. (Putting Hubby Through).

You may also have heard about some overly anxious moms who you would think were trying to earn a Ps.T. (Putting Son Through)—the Eagle program, that is.

That's not what we mean by the support of an interested family member.

To be really helpful, a parent has to use good sense and allow his or her son to earn his own Eagle. However, that parent can provide some much needed support. To do this, an understanding of the Eagle advancement program is essential. The parent, for instance, does not have to go on all the outings or participate in the service projects. Helping in these areas is great, however, even if it's only some driving now and again.

An important *key* to a Scout's advancement is that the parent or family member be aware of what the various rank advancements mean. For example, this person needs to know what must be done for a boy to earn Tenderfoot. What does the Scout have to do to accomplish this first jump toward Eagle?

Keeping the *Go For The Eagle Chart* on display at home is a big help. From it a parent can mark a calendar for the first part of June with a notation that Scotty's Life Rank is due in August. If he hasn't reached that rank in the allotted time, the parent can ask how he's doing and check with the Scoutmaster on his progress.

This type of checking and notation keeps a boy on the right track. It shows interest and support.

Often just a little reminder is all that's needed from the home front.

"Aren't you about due for Life rank, Scotty? How's it coming? Anything Mom and I can do to help?"

Sometimes, a parent may need to say to the Scoutmaster, "I don't believe Scotty has had a chance to finish his Communications Merit Badge. Can you help him with that last requirement he needs — conducting a Court of Honor? It would sure make him feel great."

Parents need to remember that it's difficult for a Scoutmaster to remember every boy's needs. There are just too many details to remember for a whole troop. Parents, however, can keep tabs on their son and see that he's moving along. Scoutmasters will appreciate the interest and support.

In Scouting, as in all other areas, a parent needs to model the characteristics he wants his son to achieve. In Scouting, the best way to do this is for the parent to get involved. Be a committee member (more later on this subject), serve enthusiastically, and then see the program take on a whole new meaning.

One dad who became a Scoutmaster himself had the following to say:

"To become Eagle Scouts, boys need to have a consistent program. Camping is a big part of the game; it's very important to the boys. We went camping once a month rain or shine. The boys' lives are busy and filled with many activities other than Scouting, so I scheduled their trips way in advance."

Leaders and parents alike need to remember this one example, out of many that could be told, of consistency and commitment to the Scouting program.

A Special Note To Parents

Scouts love receiving their beads, their merit badges, and especially their rank advancement patches. It's the responsibility of Scout leaders to see that the boys receive them. If your son is not receiving his awards soon after the work is done, talk with the Scoutmaster or bring up the problem at a Scout Committee meeting.

When Courts of Honor are held, be sure to attend these special events. It's important for a young man to have someone he loves present. The meetings usually last only an hour, and they provide much incentive to the boy.

Not just receiving these awards *but also displaying them* becomes very important to the Scout. The beads are easy for him to slip on his leather belt loop. As a Scout earns his merit badges and rank advancement patches, he wants to see them on his uniform *yesterday.* He wants others in his troop to see, by his uniform decorations, where he is in Scouting and what he's accomplished so far.

Mom or someone in the family needs to take the few minutes necessary to sew the rank advancement patch on the Scout's uniform. At first these patches change every few months. Keep the old ones on file to display elsewhere later. Six patch changes will take place, so sew the stitches on the big side. This will make it easy to put them on and take them off. The sewing for the patches only needs to be able to hold through the washing of the shirt until the next rank advancement is received.

Then there's the merit badge sash, a beautiful and effective way to display these colorful awards. As your boy brings home each badge, look it over with him. Point out to him the colorful and artistic design that represents each field of effort.

Either sew or glue the badges on the Scout's sash. Rarely, if ever, does the sash need washing, so many families prefer using Elmer's glue or a hot glue gun to secure them in place. Just place the sash on the boy, determine where his shoulder line is and begin placing the merit badges either two or three across, working down.

Display the sash in a prominent place in the home. It becomes a conversation piece and gives your son extra recognition for the work he has done. Boys like to explain what each badge means to guests and visitors. The badges are beautiful in and of themselves, and seeing them motivates the boy to keep earning more.

Also, if the sash is hanging in a permanent spot, it's not as easy to misplace. The boy can grab it as he dashes off to any formal affair such as a Court of Honor. However, the sash is generally not worn to Scout meetings or regular activities.

Another way for a parent or family member to help a Scout along the trail is to pitch in on the merit badge work. If you have an area of expertise (and most people do in the more than 100 merit badges offered), volunteer to be a merit badge counselor.

You *do* have to be approved to be a counselor. You or a member of the Committee can submit an application to the local council or district advancement committee to obtain that approval. Then your name will be on the list distributed to local leaders. You usually don't get asked to counsel that often, and you learn a lot about the Scout program.

At the very least, offer to drive on merit badge trips. Or get a couple of Scouts together to read the Constitution as they earn the Citizenship in the Nation Merit Badge. Or perhaps offer to take a few boys to a town meeting to fulfill a requirement for Citizenship in the Community.

It's important for family members to remember that *each Scouting requirement will be a benefit to the young man, his school work, his community, and his home life.* Show interest, offer encouragement, and gain an understanding of the program. Keep in mind that you will not have to spend a large amount of time, but also that no effort is too great to bring about the results obtainable from the Eagle program.

A Note To Both Leaders And Parents

It almost goes without saying, but it's an often overlooked fact. Not all boys are going to be strong in all areas of Scouting, just as adults are not strong in all areas of endeavor.

The Eagle program demands a fair amount of verbal and written skills. However, it also demands camping, hiking and sports activities. Some boys would just as soon participate only in the outdoor activities. Others would just as soon never go on an overnighter. They like the "bookwork."

The Eagle program rounds out the young men who participate in it. The boys do things they otherwise might never attempt.

Parents and leaders need to realize there will be difficult hurdles for every boy. Patience and encouragement are the key words. A little parental push now and again helps too.

Case in point: We know of a Scout who agreed to go on a 50-miler. He agreed to carry his portion of the troop supplies. However, on the day he was to leave, he decided he did not want to go. All of a sudden, there were tears and trauma.

His dad firmly said, "Son, you made a commitment. You're not sick, and there's no reason you shouldn't carry through with the plans for this hike. Your mother and I feel strongly that you need to finish what you start."

A half-hour later, when the boy had thought things over and everything was under control, he walked out the door and was on his way. Before he left, however, he looked back at his parents and said softly, "Thanks for making me go."

That hike turned out to be the greatest experience of this young man's life. Now in his early twenties, he still talks about his 50-miler.

Every Scouting leader and every informed parent works toward a vital end—helping a young person accomplish one of his first major goals in life—attaining his Eagle award. What goal could be more worthwhile, both for the young man himself and for society?

B.S.A TROOP 67

NEWS & REVIEWS April

BE PREPARED

MARK YOUR CALENDAR -
    Weekly meetings every Wednesday at 7 p.m., unless notified
    April 25 - Scout Committee Meeting - 7 p.m.
    All parents are urged to attend.

WELCOME to our new Troop Committee Chairman, MIKE WILLIS. With all the good
leaders we have at the helm, no wonder Troop 67 sweeps so many honors!

CONGRATULATIONS to the following young men who earned awards at our most recent
Troop Court of Honor:

On My Honor Award:	JEFF CRANE, ANDY GREGERSEN, ADAM GEYER
	JASON MARTY
2nd Gold Palm:	TODD ELLSWORTH
Conservation Award:	RICH HATHAWAY
1st Class:	CRAIG ELLSWORTH
Scout/Tenderfoot:	BRADY ELLSWORTH and STEVEN HATHAWAY

    We've had some busy Scouts the past several months. The Troop earned a
total of 36 merit badges. GREAT GOING, GUYS!
    Honorable mention for most merit badges earned went to CHRIS PETERSEN with
a total of six, followed by ROBBIE HOCH with five.

SCOUTS, IT PAYS TO WEAR YOUR COMPLETE UNIFORM

    A surprise uniform check at the Court of Honor won four Scouts gift
certificates to Leatherby's. In full and complete uniform were BRADY ELLSWORTH,
RYAN HILBERT, TODD JOHNSON and TRAVIS JOHNSON. AARON GREGERSEN, ANDREW
GREGERSEN and CRAIG ELLSWORTH were close runners-up. Next time, all Scouts will
have been forewarned.

LEADERS HONORED

    For many years of Scout service to the Troop, BERT ELLSWORTH was awarded
a beautiful wall plaque. Bert has recently been asked to serve as the Post
Committee Chairman.
    Also awarded certificates for service to the Troop were Assistant
Scoutmasters JACK HILBERT and JERRY AMBROSE.

COMPUTER MERIT BADGE REPORT By Ryan Hilbert

    At our last Scout function on March 20, we had a guest speaker help us
on the Computer Merit Badge. His name was Don Geyer, and he brought us
computers to see and use. We will be continuing the merit badge for one more
week and hope all Scouts will comply. We must also thank Don Geyer for his help
and supervision.

                                     Ryan Hilbert, Asst. Editor

A Look At Scouting's Organizational Structure

National Headquarters
Located in Texas

↕

Regions
Comprising large geographical areas

↕

Areas
Subdivisions of Regions

↕

Local Scout Council
The council is comprised of a number of geographical districts. The council service center is usually located in one of the larger cities in a given area.

↕

District
One of the geographical divisions in a Scout council. District Scouting executives usually work out of the council office. The District Chairmen and Commissioners are volunteer community leaders.

↕

Chartered Institutions
Usually a church, club or citizen's group. The head of each chartered institution is the executive officer.

↕

Scouting Coordinator
A local person who coordinates all Scouting groups and activities within a chartered institution.

↕

Committee Chairman (and Committee)
Coordinates the activites of an *individual Scouting group* such as the Cubs, Varsity Scouts, etc.

↕

Scoutmaster (and Assistants)

↕

Youth Leaders
Troop Guide, Senior Patrol Leader, Patrol Leaders, etc.

Family Member ← - - - - - - → **Merit Badge Counselors**
Approved by local council

Scout

With tools in hand, Scotty and a group of fellow Scouts are off on a service project.

4

Preparing For The Big One

(Making Those Service Hours Meaningful)

In Chapter 2 we looked at a bird's eye view of the Eagle step-by-step advancement process. We saw what was required for each rank. As mentioned, this information is outlined in detail in the *Official Boy Scout Handbook*.

An area that needs some further explanation for Eagle candidates is service hours. That's what this chapter is about.

Why Service Hours?

By the time Scotty Scout becomes a Star, the Eagle rank looks like a real possibility. Participating in several service projects is one of the major requirements along the way. It's here Scotty learns that he's really part of a group. He also learns that this special group gives service to the community in which he lives.

When we talk about service hours, we don't want Scotty to be thinking like Tom Sawyer. In other words, a Scout should not be pondering how he will get his patrol over to do his yard work while he sits and watches. As was mentioned, the emphasis is on *service to the community*.

As each member of the patrol moves up through the higher ranks, service hours and service projects are required for advancement. While a Star Scout, Scotty must perform six hours of service to others. As a Life Scout he must do the same. This service time may be given on an individual basis, or it may be a troop or patrol project.

When a Scout assists an Eagle candidate on his Eagle service project, the hours count toward his own individual rank advancement. *Note:* The actual Eagle Scout service project is covered in Chapter 6.

It's Easy As One, Two, Three

So just what are the steps involved in carrying out successful service projects in the Star and Life ranks? They are as easy as *One, Two, Three*:

1. First, select a project that's interesting and meaningful. The possibilities are almost endless. (See a sample list at the end of this chapter.) The work done should be for people outside the Scout's own troop and preferably outside Scouting.
2. Get Scoutmaster approval *ahead of time* for all service project work.
3. Do the work under proper supervision. And remember, of course, that no pay is to be taken for the work that's done.

That's all there is to it.

Note: The six hours required for Star and Life ranks *do not* have to be completed at one time or on one project. For example, a Scout may spend three hours helping an Eagle candidate on his project, two hours with a couple of other Scouts from his patrol doing volunteer work at their school, and one hour assisting an elderly neighbor with her yard work.

Keeping A Record Of Service Hours

Start early to keep a *Go For The Eagle* file folder. In it keep a sheet of paper titled *Go For The Eagle Service Hours.*

Every time Scotty spends an hour or two in service to others, he should write the date, the time spent and what kind of project it was. Here's an example:

Go For The Eagle Service Hours
Service Hours Since First Class was Earned

Jan. 6 - Troop cleanup project at the Community Park — 2 hours
Mar. 15 - Helped Mrs. Vogt clear her garden — 1 hour
Apr. 2 - Assisted Roger Jones on his Eagle Project — 3 hours

Total 6 hours

In the above example we see a total of six hours. Scotty Scout now has his service requirement for Star rank. He needs to begin to keep a similar record as he works toward his six hours for Life rank.

Sometimes service hours are performed, but a Scout forgets he even did the work unless he keeps the kind of notes shown above. It can be surprising just how fast service hours add up in the Star and Life ranks.

By participating in service work, Scotty Scout is preparing for his own Eagle service project. He is also making significant strides toward that all-important goal—*the Eagle.*

A List of Service Project Ideas
Community Related Ideas

Help organize a Cub Pack or a Scout Troop for handicapped children.
Collect toys for a children's home.
Organize an entertainment day for community nursing homes.
Do a project for children in other lands.
Do a painting project at a local school, church, YMCA, etc.
Conduct a safety education program in a school or nursing home.
Hold a Christmas or Easter party at a children's home or nursing home.
Do something for the needy.
Conduct a safe swim school for small children.
Collect and repair and distribute toys to needy children.
Do a landscaping project at a public or private school.
Conduct a safety related school assembly.
Construct nature trails in a park.
(Note: The BSA Supply Division has signs available.)
Do a cemetery cleanup project.
Refinish benches and tables at a community park.
Serve with community and business leaders on a special service project.
Organize a community cleanup drive.
Serve the blind as readers, guides, etc.
Honor community leaders with a ceremony.
Help set up community emergency service facilities.
Plant trees and flowers in a park or cemetery.
Take a census of conditions in public parks.
Clear a park trail.
Conduct a trail survey.
Put together a "Where to Go in Our Community" booklet.

Do landscaping work at a hospital, library, city hall, etc.
Give service to the handicapped or to those in the hospital.
Restore a historical landmark.
Organize a community blood drive.
Help new people in the community; also new citizens.
Make a historical map of the community.
Paint playground equipment at schools or parks.
Collect food for the needy and arrange distribution.
Set up and conduct a July 4th celebration.
Construct and man a tourist information booth.

Safety Related Projects

Organize a safe driving contest or put on a safe driving
  demonstration.
Conduct or take part in fire department safety
  demonstrations.
Work on home safety
  window displays.
Conduct a hazard
  hunt at schools and
  other institutions.
Conduct a lifesaving
  demonstration.
Demonstrate water
  safety in pools.
Conduct a water safety education program.
Organize hunter safety and rifle range safety
  demonstrations.
Stage a forest fire prevention demonstration.
Devise a seat belt demonstration for a public
  function.
Organize a safe boating or canoeing demonstration.
Clear dangerous and
  flammable debris
  from empty lots
  and fields.
Help stage an outdoor fire
  safety demonstration with the fire department.
Help plot a traffic map in cooperation with the
  highway department or the local police.
Conduct a survey of traffic safety.
Set up window displays on traffic safety or fire safety.
Organize a bicycle safety check.
Organize a bicycle education program.
Organize and conduct a safety poster contest.
Conduct an auto safety program.
Conduct a driver reaction testing program.
Distribute pedestrian and driver safety literature.

Sponsoring Institution Related Projects

Organize a cleanup of the area around the sponsoring
  institution.
Repair songbooks or do other service in the office.
Provide a babysitting service during adult meetings.

Refinish floors in the buildings.
Refinish furniture.
Repair equipment.
Establish a safety patrol or safety program.
Publish an institutional newsletter.
Conduct a cleanup campaign.
Set up a First Aid booth at institutional events.
Study the parking area and arrange for improvement.
Develop a plan to improve the landscaping and carry it out.
Build permanent fire pits for summer camping.
Paint rooms, garage areas, etc.
Paint trash cans and other property.
Paint playground equipment.

Conservation Related Projects

Organize school assemblies or bulletin boards featuring the BSA Outdoor Code.
Organize a "Good Outdoor Manners" demonstration for community clubs and
    organizations.
Make store window exhibits on "Keeping America Beautiful."
Carry out a wildlife habitat improvement project.
Landscape along roadways and public campsite areas.
Help in a community anti-litter campaign.
Help clean up streams and reduce erosion along river banks.
Plant ornamental and fruit trees along roads and in parks.
Construct birdhouses in public areas.
In city areas, plant and maintain window boxes and shrubbery.
Clean up vacant lots and plant grass, trees and flowers.
Plant flower gardens where needed.
Reduce roadside erosion by planting trees and shrubs.
Organize a rodent control project.
Build conservation exhibits and displays.
Organize a conservation education program for a group.
Construct a small dam to promote sport fishing.
Construct nesting boxes for birds, ducks, and other wildlife.
Plant hedgerows to protect topsoil from wind erosion and to provide food
    and protection for wildlife.
Distribute literature on clean water awareness.
Help improve woodlands by selective cutting, insect and disease control and
    fire prevention measures.
Prune and thin groves of trees.
Clean spring holes to allow water access for wildlife.
Work with the forest service on fire prevention measures.

5

For The Fun Of It

(Camping and the Great Outdoors)

So far it sounds like this business of getting to Eagle rank is all work. But not so. It's also great fun—the kind of fun just about every Scout and his leader enjoys. Outdoor Scouting experiences include everything from studying the stars to white water rapid expeditions. It's up to the boys in the patrol and their leaders to decide what kinds of outdoor activities best suit each unit.

Remember: A Scout should be a well-rounded individual.

Part of each boy's personality and skill development obviously needs to take place out of doors.

What's Required?

Required badges for Eagle in the outdoor category are:

> Camping
> and
> Personal Fitness
> *or* Swimming
> *or* Sports

Then for *elective* work Scouts have a choice of many merit badges involving nature and the great out-of-doors. Some of these include:

- Archery
- Astronomy
- Athletics
- Aviation
- Backpacking
- Bird Study
- Cooking
- Cycling
- Fishing

- Forestry
- Golf
- Hiking
- Horsemanship
- Mammals
- Motorboating
- Nature
- Oceanography
- Orienteering
- Photography
- Plant Science
- Rowing
- Skiing
- Small-Boat Sailing
- Water Skiing

Note: None of the above *elective* outdoor-oriented merit badges are required for Eagle. However, for a Scout who likes outdoor activities, these badges offer a wide variety of choices.

The Fabulous "Fifty Miler"
A.K.A. "The Fifty-Blister"

Although not required for Eagle rank, one of the highlights of any Scouting career is the fabulous "Fifty-miler" (also known as "The Fifty-blister"). This event almost always takes place as a hike. However, there are also events such as a 50-mile canoe trip which are referred to as a "Fifty-miler."

The 50-mile hike is often said to "turn a boy into a man." All the skills learned in the Hiking Skill Award, and all the shorter preparatory hikes lead up to this "man-sized adventure."

Boys who make the sad mistake of choosing ill-fitting hiking boots only remember sore feet and pain. A Scout will know whether or not he has followed the motto, "Be Prepared." He'll know it when he's just a short way into his fifty-mile Scouting experience.

However, boys with blisters and others living with unwise choices in clothing and food almost always "hang in there" and finish the trek. In spite of errors in planning, they go on to complete what for some becomes a true ordeal.

A few Scouts need reminding that they can't take along all the comforts of home. Overpacking can be as bad as underpacking. And no dirt bikes or ghetto blasters are allowed on this or any other hike. Sorry, boys.

Most Scouts remember their fifty-miler as their most memorable Scouting event. They talk about feeling close to nature, close to fellow Scouts who share the trek, and close to their Scout leaders through this unique experience.

Again, the fifty-miler is *not* a requirement for Eagle rank. It is discussed here because all the days and nights on the trail count toward the Camping merit badge which *is* required. Requirements for Cooking and other merit badges may also be earned while on the fifty-mile experience.

Don't Forget Scout Camp

A yearly Scout camp is available to most Scouts around the world. Boys need to sign up several months in advance for this week-long activity. The local council supplies all the basic information.

The important thing to remember about Scout camp is not only the fun it offers but the fact that it can give Scotty Scout a big boost toward Eagle rank. Why? Simply because at camp excellent leaders are available to teach and train Scouts in a concentrated environment. At camp it's possible to earn as many as six or seven merit badges, depending on how hard a boy wants to work.

Usually it's best for a Scout to concentrate on four or five badges at most. He then allows time for the fun part of camping. Many Scouts attend camp several years in a row. Each time they go they are able make more progress toward their Eagle.

Attention: Scoutmasters

A few reminders will make for a more successful camping experience for most troops:

- Meet with all the boys who plan to attend camp. Find out what each Scout wants to do at camp. Learn what merit badges he would like to earn while he is there.
- Be sure the boys who want to work for merit badges have the individual pamphlets and any needed material well ahead of time.
- Advise the boys not to overschedule themselves. Some will only want to go to camp to have fun. Others will want to come home with a fistful of merit badges. Let them know the merit badges that are especially fun to earn. These would include Basketry, Archery, Rifle Shooting, Indian Lore, and Canoeing, to name just a few. Also offered are badges sometimes difficult to finish at home, such as the challenging Environmental Science merit badge. It can be a "bear," and it's on the required list for Eagle.

Almost every Scout wants to return home a "hero" of sorts. He wants to say he made it through Wilderness Survival or he shivered his way through the cold waters of the mile swim. All leaders should make it a point to see that Scout camp is a happy and rewarding memory for each Scout who attends.

Keep a Record of All Overnighters

It's very important to keep a record of each overnight outing. Since the Camping merit badge is required for Eagle, verification of at least 20 overnighters is essential.

In his *Go For The Eagle* file folder suggested in Chapter 4, Scotty Scout needs to keep another sheet of paper called "Camping Record."

All he needs is to be sure to write something like the following after each campout:

Go For The Eagle
Scotty's Camping Record

	Days	Nights
August 12-13 - Overnight Troop Campout (Spring Meadow)	2	1
Sept. 2-3-4 - Weekend Council Campout (Wright's Lake)	3	2

Start this record with the very first campout. With this information on hand, there will be no question about the number of days and nights spent when it's time to pass off the Camping merit badge.

Limitless Activities

The list of outdoor Scouting experiences could go on and on. It's all up to the imagination and interests of the boys and the patrol leadership. The important thing to remember is that this can be one of the most memorable and truly "fun" parts of the Boy Scout program.

It's also a vital part of the requirements necessary for Eagle rank.

And ah, yes, camping can be a memorable experience for Scout leaders, as well. As one Scoutmaster related:

"I guess I was a bit naive when I went on my first campout with the boys. I thought I'd just sit around the campfire while the boys did the cooking and cleanup.

"As I sat watching the breakfast cooking taking place, the first thing I saw emerge from the fire was a brown/black blob of something the boys called 'scrambled eggs.' Next came round objects not discernible until I saw the boys pour some maple syrup on them. And then came an elongated piece of something on a stick that was burning profusely. I later found out it was bacon. Imagine, flaming bacon for breakfast!

"As I hurriedly proceeded to prepare my own breakfast, I began to wonder how the cleanup procedure would be handled. You guessed it—the boys used the old Indian/pioneer method. They spread all the dirty dishes and pans out in the open and then prayed for rain. A few just hoped some animals would come along and lick their platters clean."

What an experience! This Scout leader, along with many others, had much to learn about Scouts and their camping habits.

Summer and winter scout camping give life-long memories plus *merit badges and other Eagle advancement requirements.*

6

The All-Important Eagle Service Project

After helping and observing on many service projects in the past, the Eagle candidate is now ready to "solo."

Where to begin?

First, follow the guidelines supplied by the local Boy Scout council offices. Most have a worksheet for the Scout to fill in and submit with his Eagle papers.

Keep a Calendar

Next, and very important is a single sheet of paper labeled GO FOR THE EAGLE PROJECT CALENDAR. *This cannot be stressed enough.* As soon as Scotty Scout first begins to fill in his Eagle Project Worksheet, he should keep a calendar of the dates and times of everything he does. This calendar should be kept in his *Go For The Eagle* file folder along with his camping record and other Eagle information. An example of a project calendar follows:

Scotty Scout says, "Finally I get to organize and supervise my own Eagle Service Project."

S A M P L E
Eagle Project Calendar

January 18

I discussed several Eagle project ideas with my Scoutmaster—1/2 hour

Called the Recruiting Center of the Blood Bank about setting up a blood drive - 15 minutes

January 23

Called the local high school about using the school for the blood drive. Was told they had no dates available - 5 minutes

February 2

Called the County offices asking about possible project and was told what they had available - 10 minutes

February 2

Discussed the possible project ideas with my Scoutmaster. We decided I should take on one of the County projects— building encasements for drinking fountains along a bike trail - 5 minutes.

February 6

Called the County Park Ranger to set up the water fountain project I had chosen - 10 minutes

February 15

The Park Ranger called back and said the project was "go" for March 10. He told me what the County would supply and what I would need to supply - 10 minutes.

February 22

Made up flyers for the boys in my Scout troop - 30 minutes

February 26

Distributed the flyers to the Scouts - 30 minutes

March 4

Scouted the park area where I was to do the project to plan it roughly. I received District approval. - 30 minutes

March 7

I received the signatures from the Unit Committee Representative and from my Scoutmaster - 15 minutes

March 8

I called McDonald's about some drink syrup and supplies - 15 minutes

March 9

Purchased cement and fireclay that I needed. In the evening I called the Scouts to remind them what to bring and when to be ready for the project - 60 minutes

March 10

Picked up the McDonald's drink and also some film for my camera. Started and completed the Eagle project - 6 hours

March 11

Went back to do a final cleanup and to polish the river rocks on the fountains. - 2 hours

March 12

Wrote up my report and also some thank you notes to people who helped.

Without an accurate calendar, the written report of the project becomes an extremely difficult assignment. With it, the written report is a snap.

But, let's not concern ourselves about the write-up just yet. First, we need to determine what this special project is going to be. After all, it's only going to take place once in a lifetime, and everyone involved wants it to be a positive experience.

To begin, Scotty Scout must have completed all his requirements for Life rank. Then the Eagle Project calendar begins.

It's important to remember that the Eagle Project is different from all the other service projects the Scout has participated in so far. The key words for this one are *plan, develop and give leadership to* a project that is *helpful to your religious institution, school or town.*

Selecting a Project

Scotty Scout, now an Eagle candidate, begins the planning stage of his project. Almost always he enlists the help of his Scoutmaster and other adults. Thinking creatively, he comes up with several project ideas that interest him. On his calendar

he writes down the actual date of this planning session and how much time he spent.

There are literally hundreds, maybe thousands, of possible project ideas. Here is a list of just a few possibilities. Other ideas can be found in the list of general service projects at the end of Chapter 4 some of which may also be used as Eagle projects.

Painting playground equipment at a school
Organizing a blood drive
Restoration of an historical site
Refinishing tables and benches in a park or at a school
Repairing restrooms or drinking fountains at a public site
Organizing a community CPR/rescue seminar
Landscaping a church site
Building permanent fire pits
Building a YMCA daycamp site
Making and distributing first aid kits for needy families
Providing winter feed for endangered animals
Repairing hymn books for a church
Organizing a community cleanup project

Scotty Scout may want to check with local schools, churches, community recreation and park districts, and public agencies such as the county in which he lives. People in these organizations are many times very willing to help. They will sometimes supply not only ideas but materials and supervisory assistance for an Eagle project.

Phone calls to leaders in various organizations are an excellent learning experience for a Scout. He should record on his project calendar the date and the time he spends on each call.

Then Scotty and his Scoutmaster must make a final selection. The project chosen should be one that's realistic for the boy and his troop to carry out.

Projects that *Do Not* Qualify

Keep in mind that there are projects that will *not* qualify for an Eagle service project. These would include:

* Anything involving Boy Scouts of America activities or troop or council property.
* Routine labor normally done on a volunteer basis. An Eagle project has to show planning, creativity, and the supervision of several people other than the candidate.
* Projects for profit-making organizations. For example, painting the outside of a nursing home would benefit the owner who is making a profit. On the other hand, organizing an "Entertainment Day" for the residents of the nursing home would benefit the people in the home instead.
* Projects where two or more Eagles participate. Only one Eagle may qualify for one individual project. Two cannot qualify for the same project.
* Projects not approved ahead of time by the proper people.
* Any project that requires completion *after* the Eagle Board of Review. All work must be done before the Board of Review.
* Projects started *before* the candidate has completed Life Scout rank.

And no, Scotty, sorry but decorating the house or gym for a big Scout party will not qualify, either.

Getting Approval

The next step is getting the project approved. The Scoutmaster's signature is needed, along with the signature of a representative from the unit committee and a representative from the local district or council.

There are occasions when the person responsible for district or council approval may live a long way from the Eagle candidate. If this is the case, check to see if this person can give telephone approval. Scotty can then just write in the leader's name on the appropriate line of his project worksheet along with his own initials. Add "phone approval" in parentheses along with the date.

Many local troop committees require the Eagle candidate to appear before the committee. This, of course, would be at a committee meeting preceding the actual project. The Scout should be in full uniform to present his Eagle project idea to the group for their approval. If approved, this is a good time for Scotty Scout to ask a unit committee representative for his or her signature on the project worksheet.

Again, he makes a note on his calendar when each of these steps is done.

It's vital to have all three approval signatures before the project begins. This gives the Scout full authorization to proceed. It also eliminates any chance that a project might be disapproved because of a technicality later on.

Onward Into The Project

The decision is made. The date of the project has been set. Now what?

Invitations! Everyone likes to receive an invitation. This is a great way to encourage others to be a part of this special event. Scotty will want to create an attractive format. He'll need to be sure it includes all the pertinent information. Invitations may be either handwritten, typed or quick-printed for distribution.

Scotty should send or deliver his invitations at least a week or two before the actual project date. Boys at this age forget easily, so it's wise not to send them too early.

Scotty will want to keep a copy of the invitation to be included with the project write-up. He should also be sure he adds to his project calendar the time he spends preparing and distributing his invitations.

As the actual date nears, Scotty must note what needs to be done on the days preceding the project. What supplies must be bought? Who does he need to contact? Are a camera and film available and ready to take photos? Have plans been made for serving a drink or refreshments?

DATE.... **JANUARY 5**

Thursday

<u>Time</u> : 9:00 A.M.
Completion

<u>Place</u> : Carnegie School

<u>What</u> : Travis J. Eagle Project

We Will be Assembling, Preparing and Cementing Benches on the School Grounds.

<u>Wear</u> : Work Clothes

<u>Bring</u> : Shovel

<u>Lunch</u> : Pizza and Drink Provided (For those who work 9-12:00)

This Will Count for Your Service Hours !!

Please, Do Not Bring Skateboards.

An attractive invitation/project announcement flyer helps to get other Scouts to work on an Eagle project.

Here's how a Scout might schedule the final week before his actual project date:

Monday - Be sure all materials are ready.

Tuesday - Buy film for camera.

Wednesday - Have bags and rags ready for cleanup.

Thursday - Check with the people in charge to be sure everything is in order.

Friday - *Make reminder calls to everyone about the date and time of the project.*

Saturday - PROJECT DAY!

The Big Day Arrives

With proper prior planning, the project day should go smoothly. Occasionally an outdoor project must be rescheduled due to bad weather. However, barring any unforeseen circumstances, Scotty Scout is ready for his exercise in leadership.

A "Sign-in/Sign-out" sheet is a great way to keep track of who actually participates in the project. Some people will come late and leave early. This sheet allows the Scout an easy way to keep a record of who helped on the project. He can also tell how many hours were spent on the work.

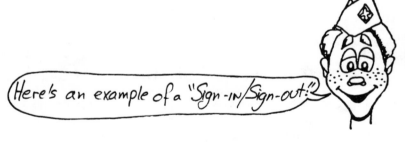

Here's an example of a "Sign-in/Sign-out:"

Scotty Scout's Eagle Project
SIGN-IN/SIGN-OUT SHEET

Helper's Name	Time Arrived	Time Left
Jim Case, Scoutmaster	8:00 a.m.	4:30 p.m.
Joe Jones	8:00 a.m.	10:00 a.m.
Billy Burger	8:30 a.m.	4:30 p.m.
Harry Hornblower	9:00 a.m.	4:00 p.m.

Once into the project, Scotty should follow the plans he outlined in his project worksheet. This is when he learns to follow a plan of action. He has noted who is to do what, and when, and where it's to be done. Now he needs to supervise the group and see that his plan is put into effect.

Scotty, like all Eagle candidates, helps on the project. However, his main concern should be *leadership* and *supervision*. He needs to check each group involved and be sure they know what they are to do. He must give correction when needed. He also needs to give praise and encouragement as the work proceeds. A Scouting leader should be on hand to check and be sure everything is being done correctly.

One Eagle candidate made this observation in his project write-up: "I learned that there are workers and there are shirkers." Many young men have their first experience with "workers and shirkers" on their Eagle project. How they handle both groups means a great deal in this leadership experience. Obviously, the young man in charge needs to praise the workers. He also needs to encourage the shirkers to get busy and do their job. It's all part of the learning experience.

Most Eagle projects require working at least several hours and many times, more than one day. Some Scouts provide refreshments during the project or after it is completed. This, of course, is optional. However, refreshments for boys this age are an incentive and more Scouts are likely to attend if there's a promise of something to eat.

Note on refreshments: We know it's hard to imagine, but young Scouts have been known to show up for an Eagle project just as it nears its end. They come at this particular time knowing this is when the goodies are usually served. Hard to believe, isn't it?

Some Eagle candidates go so far as to establish a "no work, no eat" policy, asking an adult supervisor to enforce it. Others have fooled everyone and served the refreshments at the beginning of the project. These boys have then had to handcuff everyone to a tree to be sure they don't leave after eating.

Some fast food restaurants provide big coolers with ice. They usually charge only a nominal fee for soft drink syrup. However, arrangements need to be made in advance. This can be a refreshing treat on a hot day. The Eagle candidate should at least see there is access to drinking water for his helpers.

The Finishing Touches

Once the project is done, cleanup is mandatory. Always allow time for this part of the project. The area of the project must be left in excellent condition, and the Eagle candidate is responsible to see that this is done.

Soon after completion, the Scout fills in the final page of his worksheet listing the project date, who participated, and any changes that took place in the original planning. Last, but certainly not least, thank you notes should be sent to everyone who helped. This would, of course, include members of the troop, the Scoutmaster, and any community leaders involved. Thank you notes be as simple as a short note saying:

> Dear_____,
> Thank you for your help on my Eagle Scout Service Project. It was all completed on schedule, and I received a letter from the Park Ranger praising everyone's efforts.
> Your help was much appreciated.
> Sincerely,
> Scott Scout

With this final step, the Eagle candidate can feel a big sense of accomplishment. He has demonstrated leadership and the ability to serve his community in a meaningful way.

At last, the coveted Eagle rank is now within easy reach!

Something To Think About

Much is said about our national resources, but the outpouring of volunteer labor performed by the Boy Scouts is seldom considered. However, when close to 25,000 Eagle projects are completed in a given year which involve nearly 150,000 Scouts logging almost 300,000 hours in community service, the figures become significant.

It would be interesting to calculate all the work done by the Boy Scouts of America, and particularly the work done by those involved in Eagle projects. The savings to the community would no doubt be in the millions of dollars.

Eagle candidates and Scouts, in general, can be proud of their contribution to their schools, their churches, and the towns in which they live.

7

The Project Writeup

(How to Jump the Big Hurdle)

Happy Day! The project's completed. Now it's time for the written report. Almost everybody's reaction is, "Uggh!" It seems a natural tendency to avoid this part of the Eagle process like the plague.

One dad was overheard telling his boy, "No, son, we can't go out and hire a secretary to do this for you. You have to do it yourself."

It's a fact that the project write-up often delays more Eagle candidates than any other part of the process. Most boys just do not know how to go about it or even where to begin.

But don't despair. The material in this chapter will be a *big* help. And the item that will be the biggest help of all will be the *Go For The Eagle Project Calendar* that was stressed in Chapter 6.

Do It While It's Fresh

Important: Do the write-up as soon as possible after the project.

The longer it's put off, the harder it is to remember all the details, and the more difficult the procedure becomes.

To make the process quick and easy, here's what to do —

First, go back to the Eagle Scout Service Project Worksheet supplied by the local council. This will provide much of the background information for the write-up.

After the worksheet is filled in completely, it's time to get out that important *Go For the Eagle Project Calendar* you've been keeping.

Seven Easy Steps

These are the easy steps to follow:

1. Going by the calendar of dates, start writing—in complete sentences—everything that was done on each date. Give the names of people who helped, and describe each step in detail. This part of the report may take several paragraphs. The rest of the items could be just one paragraph each.

2. Next, Scotty Scout needs to "sell" himself and his completed project. He must convince the reviewer that this Eagle project was put together by the best-organized Scout in the council. Over the years, Scouts learn a great deal about leadership. They know how to get things done and how to motivate other people. Now is the time to show the reviewer that all this knowledge was put to use in this particular Eagle project.

3. Tell what was learned about other people during the project. Tell how individuals were coordinated into groups, if this applies. Did everyone follow directions? Were they supportive? Did the Eagle candidate have any major problems with anyone and why?

4. Tell how much time was spent *by the Eagle candidate* and how much time was spent *by those who helped*. List the hours and totals. Use the Sign-in/Sign-out sheet and the calendar discussed in the last chapter. These will make the calculations very easy.

5. Write details about any cleanup procedures that were necessary. Tell what had to be taken care of after the project. This might include such things as returning the next day for a final check, getting supplies back to their proper owners, cleaning paint brushes or tools, etc.

6. List any changes that occurred in the total planning of the project. This might include: not having as many people attend as planned, weather problems, one or two people who did not follow directions, and finishing well ahead of (or way behind) schedule. Tell how any of the changes or problems were handled.

7. Last, but not least, be sure to include a short paragraph expressing appreciation to leaders who gave special help and

support. A few words of thanks to parents or family members who assisted is also an excellent idea.

Do a Draft First, Then The Final Copy

A typewritten or computer-produced report is best, of course. However, if a typewriter or word processor is not available, a neat, handwritten report is acceptable. The average length is about three to five pages (double-spaced, if typed).

Be sure to do a final check for spelling and neatness. Some Eagle applications are returned for these two reasons alone. Eliminate this needless delay. *Proofread carefully.* Ask someone to double-check grammar and accuracy.

Sketches and Photos

If appropriate, include a sketch of the area where the project was done. Add anything that will give the reviewers a better idea of what the project was. Include a copy of any paperwork such as invitations or letters of acknowledgment from community organizations, etc.

Photos are also great. They provide an excellent history of this important event.

The Eagle project write-up and copies of your photos are used by local Scout officials only. None of this information will be sent to the National Office. All that is used at National Headquarters is the brief description of the project on the Eagle application form.

Sure glad that's done!

However, the write-up is very important at the local level. If it is not done properly, it will delay the Eagle application process.

A project write-up checklist *and* a sample of a completed Eagle Scout project write-up are shown on the next few pages.

Look these over carefully. Then get busy and start doing your own write-up. Try to get it finished within ten days of the project date. When you're done, one of the toughest hurdles will have been jumped. From now on it's all downhill.

Project Write-up Checklist

_____ Start with the Eagle Scout Project Worksheet provided by the local council service center. Fill this in completely. Be sure no dates or signatures are missing.

_____ Use the Eagle Project Calendar and the Worksheets to help with the written report.

_____ Review the next few pages in this book for a sample of a completed Eagle project write-up. Also review the write-up suggestions in this chapter.

_____ Do a rough draft first. Then rework and correct it. Then do the final copy.

_____ Check each page for proper spelling and grammar.

_____ Ask two or three people to proofread the write-up.

_____ Re-type any pages that need corrections.

_____ Check for neatness.

_____ Include photos of the project. These will be returned.

_____ Attach the write-up and photos to the Eagle application form.

Note: Remember, the write-up is used by local officials only. It will not be sent to the national office with your Eagle application. There is a place on the application for a brief description of the project.

SAMPLE PROJECT WRITE-UP

Selection Of My Project

After earning my twenty-one required merit badges, I began to look for interesting and beneficial Eagle projects. I discussed several ideas with my Scoutmaster and decided to do a blood drive. So I called the Recruiting Center of the Blood Bank about setting up one. They told me to find a facility, and they would be happy to help. I called my local high school, but they told me no dates were available, and I could not locate any other good facilities. So I decided to select a different project.

I then called the local county offices and asked if they had any work that might be filled by an Eagle service project. The man I talked with told me about two projects: building encasements for drinking fountains and cleaning up a horse trail. The fountain project appealed to me, so I called and talked it over with my Scoutmaster and then called Bill Walker, the Park Ranger, to set up the tentative project date.

Development Of Project

Later in the week I called Mr. Walker and we agreed on March 10. He told me the County would supply the sand and river rock. I was to supply the cement and fireclay. He told me to read up on cement and masonry work to get a feel for the work I would be doing. I gave him some rough sketches and plans, and he said I was doing great. On February 22, I made up a flyer to remind the Scouts in my troop about the project. I distributed these flyers to the Scouts on February 26.

On March 4, I scouted the lower parking area near the bridge to make more plans for my project. I also received approval from the District on that same date. On March 7, I received the approval signatures from my Unit Committee Representative and my Scoutmaster. That evening at my Scout meeting, I reminded the boys of my project and told them the details. I also gave them each a printed sheet of paper with details of the project. I told them I would call them and remind them the night before the project.

On March 8, I called McDonald's about some drink syrup and told them it was for an Eagle Scout project. They gave me a Scout discount on enough syrup for 100 servings, plus cups and a cooler.

The next day I went to a local lumber dealer and bought two 90-pound bags of cement and a 50-pound bag of fireclay. That evening I called the Scouts to remind them what to bring and when to be at my home. I arranged to have a wheelbarrow, three shovels, chicken wire, cement and fireclay at the work site.

The Project

On the day of the project, March 10, I went to McDonald's to pick up the syrup and supplies and also purchased some film for our family camera. I got home just as the other Scouts were arriving at 10 a.m. The rest of the day of my project went as follows:

10:00-10:30	We traveled to the park area and began setting up.
10:30- 1:00	We all worked in a system. Two mixed cement, three picked out the rocks and brought them over to where we were working, and the rest put the rocks into place. Two of the Scouts had to leave for a baseball game at lunchtime.
1:00	We finished the first drinking fountain.
1:30 - 2:30	We began the second fountain. One new Scout arrived.
2:30 - 2:45	We took a break to eat lunch.
2:45 - 3:30	We finished the second fountain.
3:30 - 4:15	We all went for some ice cream cones. I thanked the Scouts for helping me on the project.

Next Day:

    10:00-12:30   My brother and my Dad and I went back for a final inspection and to wash down the drinking fountains.

People Who Assisted on the Project

SCOUTS

Greg Jones	Todd Hansen
Ryan Scott	Travis Geyer
David Benson	Adam Ralls
Nathan Boehm	Andrew Marty
Aaron Carter	Jason Gregerson

ADULTS

Ron Ellsworth	Bill Wagner
Dean Smith	Bert Klopfer

Materials Used on the Project

wheelbarrow	chickenwire
shovels	cement
fireclay	sand
river rock	water

Hours Spent on the Project

Setting up project with park ranger	1 hour
Researching project and making plans	1 hour
Buying supplies	1 hour
Filling in worksheets	1 hour
Contacting Scouts	1 hour
Presenting project to Committee	1/2 hour
Project	5 hours
Final Inspection	1/2 hour
Write-up	4 hours
Hours Spent (By Helpers)	80 hours
Hours Spent (By Me)	16 hours
TOTAL EAGLE SERVICE PROJECT HOURS	96 hours

What did I learn from this project? I learned many things about different kinds of people. I learned that some Scouts are hard workers and some are shirkers. I also learned that some Scouts are very good at serving under a leader while some are rude. I was very, very grateful to whose who came to help me and who didn't complain. I will be sure to help them on their projects.

I now realize that many boys never make Eagle because of the last big service project. The hours spent on everything takes up time that some boys just are not willing to spend. I am glad I had the support of my parents and my family members. They really helped me a lot, and so did my Scout leaders. The project gave me leadership experience which I know will be of help to me in the future.

Additional Information on the Actual Project

When we arrived at the park area, the fountains were made of corrugated pipe. They looked very unattractive. They were also vulnerable to vandals and had been damaged many times.

I had several boys start mixing cement while two others placed chicken wire around the first fountain. This was meant to hold the cement and river rock in place.

First, we laid down a layer of cement about four inches high starting at ground level. Then we placed river rocks in the cement. Next, we placed another layer of cement and more river rock gradually tapering the cement and rocks in toward the fountain so that the base was wider than the top. Each layer took approximately fifteen minutes.

There were about ten layers. We took turns with different boys and adults working on each layer while the others continued to mix cement and gather rocks, so we had a system going all the time.

After we got to the top of the fountain, we molded a layer in to finish it off. Then we built a small step at the bottom of the fountain for small children.

The first fountain took about two-and-a-half hours to complete with everyone working. We all took a short break and started on the second fountain which took about the same time as the first one.

   The next day my brother, my father and I went back to wash away the excess cement and polish the rocks to give the fountains a finished look. They were both in good shape and were already being used by the public.

Eagle Scout Service Project
March 25

Photos I took of the two encased fountains after the project was completed. Lower Sunrise Bridge Area—American River Bike Trail.

Bike trail cyclists stopped to say they appreciated what we were doing as we built the encasements.

Work begins.

Chicken wire goes in place. Ranger Bill Wagner assisting.

Mid afternoon. Second fountain finished.

Ice-Cream Treats for everyone.

Next day scrubbing, rinsing and polishing river rock.

Dad and brother help on final cleanup.

Scotty is filling out the final papers. It won't be long now till it's all complete.

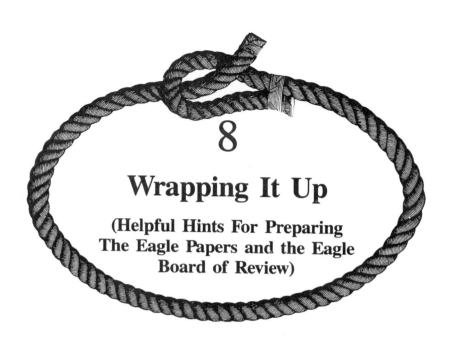

8

Wrapping It Up

(Helpful Hints For Preparing The Eagle Papers and the Eagle Board of Review)

"Oh, no. Not more paperwork!"

That's what you'll hear from most Scouts.

But don't despair. Once the Eagle project and write-up are complete, the worst is over. Now it's just a matter of filling out *one more form*—the official Eagle Scout application.

The process is not difficult. Just pick up a current application form at the local council service center and fill in the blanks.

Making It All a Little Easier

A few important words of advice:

Be certain all blanks are filled in carefully and accurately. Dates are especially important.

Also, be sure each date makes sense. This is where the Scout's one-page *Go For The Eagle Chart* will be extremely helpful. The dates on this sheet can be checked against the ones recorded in the back of the Scout's *Official Boy Scout Handbook*.

If any discrepancies occur, check with the person in charge of advancement on the troop committee. It may also be necessary to check the troop advancement forms on file in the local council service center. This would only need to be done if any advancement forms are missing in the troop records. Again, if careful records have been kept by the troop committee and by the Scout, this part of the process goes very quickly.

It's a good idea to have two application forms—one to draft in pencil and the other for a final copy. The final "official" set should be typed, if at all possible.

As mentioned in the last chapter, Scotty Scout may want to include photos with his Eagle papers. They will only be seen at the local council level. Photos are encouraged because they help the reviewers see what the project was like. Just as important, the Scout will enjoy looking back and seeing what he accomplished. It's fun to have a visual record of the project and the people who helped.

Letters of Recommendation

Some councils require them. Some do not. When they are required, it's just a matter of the Eagle candidate making a phone call or writing a note to request them—usually from 1) the Scout's school principal or counselor, 2) his parents, 3) his Scoutmaster and 4) a religious leader. The letter from a religious leader is generally optional.

Scotty should include the following information in his request:
- State that the letter should be addressed to the Boy Scouts of America.
- Say when he needs the letter to be finished.
- If the person is not sure about what to write, the Scoutmaster may have some previous letters on file. Scotty would have to make these available to the person who needs the information.
- Tell the person that the letter will be picked up when it is ready.

Submitting the Eagle Papers

Once everything is filled in and ready to go, the Scout needs to clip all his papers together with a big paperclip. Or he may choose to place his papers in a flexible, lightweight notebook. Clear plastic folders are also handy.

A photocopy of the papers should be made and kept by the Scout before they are submitted to the local council service center. This is important—there have been occasions where Eagle papers have been lost or misplaced during processing. This is rare, but one young man had to wait almost eight weeks while his application was at the council level because his papers had been misfiled.

Once the candidate's papers are complete, it's time to set up the Eagle Board of Review.

That Last Big Board of Review

A Scout may choose to have his Eagle Board of Review con-
ducted in one of three ways. He and his Scoutmaster should
decide which is best:

1) He may choose to have it held in his own troop with a council or district representative in attendance.

OR

2) The Board of Review may be set up by the district advancement committee. The Scout must contact this committee for a date.

OR

3) Eagle Boards of Review may also be held on a council
   level. These are scheduled periodically, and the Scout must
   make arrangements to attend. Usually the council will notify
   the Scout by mail of the appropriate date.

A typical Board of Review might be held in the home of a
Scout leader or in the room of a sponsoring church. Attending
would be the Scout, his parent(s), a district leader and two or
three local Scout leaders. If the Board of Review is held on
a district or council level, the meeting would generally be held
in a conference room at council headquarters.

When the Scout attends this final Board of Review, *he must
be on time and in full uniform.* He should be prepared to repeat
the Scout Oath, Law, slogan, motto. The Board may ask how
he is showing Scout spirit. He may be asked about his favorite
merit badges. And he should be prepared to tell about his Eagle service project.

As he comes to his Eagle Board of Review, Scotty Scout
should be aware that he may be asked questions such as these:

- What are your plans for the future?
- What kind of work would you like to go into?
- Do you have a part-time job to earn money?
- What part of Scouting have you liked best?
- What merit badges did you like best and why?
- Which ones did you like least and why?
- What does it mean to you to be an Eagle Scout?
- What are your plans now in Scouting?

- Do you feel being an Eagle Scout will affect your future? In what way?
- Tell about your service project. Who did it benefit? Was it a good experience for you?
- What does it mean for a Scout to "Be Prepared?"
- Do you feel you are doing your "Duty to God?" How?
- Do you honestly try to do a good turn daily?
- What is an example of a "good turn?"

If Scotty Scout has been successful thus far in his Scouting career, this Board of Review should be almost a formality. He just needs to remember to present himself in a confident, pleasant manner and to speak clearly and distinctly.

At the conclusion of the Board of Review, the Eagle candidate needs to remember to thank those who have taken their time to conduct this meeting in his behalf. He or his Scoutmaster should also be sure the final signatures are all on his Eagle application at this time.

Someone needs to be sure the Eagle papers are submitted to the council once the Board of Review is complete. This is usually the responsibility of the Scoutmaster or the committee member in charge of advancement. The Eagle papers include:

- The completed and signed Eagle Scout application.
- The Eagle service project write-up.
- Letters of recommendation, if required.
- A properly completed Advancement Report.

Sometimes the council office will return the papers to the Eagle candidate specifying that everything is complete except for one particular item. The reviewers may want the papers re-done because of spelling or appearance. A messy, penciled-in set of papers will almost certainly be returned. The Eagle candidate should take extra care to see that everything is complete, neat and accurate before submission. Then these other problems will not develop.

The Final Approval

The papers are first checked and approved at the council level. If everything is in order, the application is signed by the Scout executive and then forwarded to the National Offices of the B.S.A. Here all signatures and dates are checked. Any discrepancies will cause the papers to be returned.

If everything is approved at the National Office, the Eagle papers and the Eagle certificate are returned to the council service center.

For Scotty Scout, it's just a matter of waiting. It's a process much like a mother waiting for a baby to be born. She knows it will be coming for sure. She just doesn't know the exact day.

Scotty knows he'll need to allow *at least* several weeks and sometimes longer for his papers to be processed at the National Office. He should not schedule his Eagle Court of Honor until they are returned. It's best to check with the local council service center to see approximately how long it will take. *Be patient*. The hard part's all over.

SPECIAL NOTE: If there is a need for a rush on processing the Eagle papers, they may be sent by Federal Express or U.S. Postal Service Express Mail to the National Boy Scout Office. Applications received in express envelopes are given priority treatment.

CHECKLIST FOR EAGLE APPLICATION PAPERS AND PROCEDURES

_____ Official Eagle application form is completed. All dates and signatures are checked.

_____ Eagle Project *worksheets* are in order. All dates and signatures are complete.

_____ The Eagle Project *writeup* is complete. The Project writeup should include the following:

_____ The explanation of the project as (described in Chapter 7).

_____ Copy of the Eagle Project calendar.

_____ Copy of the invitation sent to the members of the troop.

_____ Copy of thank you notes sent to those who helped.

_____ Photocopies of any pictures that might help clarify what the project actually was.

_____ Copy of any letter(s) received from the organization that benefited from the Eagle project.

_____ Letters of recommendation, if required by the council:

_____ School principal or counselor

_____ Parent(s)

_____ Scoutmaster

_____ Religious leader (usually optional)

_____ *Make a copy of all paperwork in case the original is lost or damaged.*

_____ Hold the Eagle Board of Review.

_____ Send or personally deliver the Eagle papers to the council service center.

_____ Wait for approval from National Scout Headquarters *before* scheduling the Eagle Court of Honor.

9

Worth It All

(Planning a Memorable Court of Honor)

It's here at last. Papers have been approved locally and at National Scout Headquarters. A call comes from the council office saying the Eagle certificate and presentation kit are ready to be picked up.

It's time to prepare for the big event—the Eagle Scout Court of Honor. This will be just one of the many rewards for the years of effort Scotty Scout has put forth.

It's wise for the Scout, his parents and his Scout leaders to all be involved in the planning process. However, this is often the time when everyone says, "How do we begin the planning for this kind of affair?"

First, a date is set. Weekday evenings are popular; the night of the regular troop meeting may be used. The scheduling is all very flexible. Some Courts of Honor are held on Sundays following church meetings. Others are scheduled to coincide with an end-of-week activity. Whatever suits the Eagle candidate and the troop leadership is fine.

The Plans Begin

Lotsa things to plan and prepare.

Plans need to begin well enough ahead to include the following details:

The Eagle presentation kit mentioned earlier includes: the Eagle uniform patch, the Eagle pin for the Scout, the mother's pin and the father's tie tack. It must be picked up and paid for at the council service center. This is usually done when the Eagle papers and certificate are picked up. Sometimes the troop pays for the kit. Sometimes local service organizations pay for part of it. The Scoutmaster can usually advise on how this is handled in each area.

Whenever the kit is purchased, it's a good time to also buy invitations, program covers and possibly napkins with the Eagle emblem for the Court of Honor. Plain red, white or blue napkins may also be used. Most all Scout Trading Posts have these supplies.

Some troops like to coordinate the red, white and blue theme in decorating a serving area—tablecloth, napkins, punch, cups, etc. It's good to think ahead about refreshments and to remember simplicity is best.

If two or more Scouts have their Court of Honor at the same time, the expenses can be shared by those involved.

Photographs

Photos of the Eagle candidate are important. Some photography studios provide a free black and white photo which may be used in the Court of Honor program as well as in a news release. Polaroids also work very well for this purpose. The Scout should, of course, be photographed with his uniform, neckerchief and merit badge sash.

Color pictures are great to have and can either be done professionally or by a friend who takes color prints and slides. If a professional studio does the photos, be sure to make an appointment well in advance as it may take up to six weeks to get the finished product.

And don't forget the camera the day of the actual Court of Honor.

Invitations

Eagle Court of Honor invitations need to be filled in and sent. These may be purchased from the local council office, or the Scout may wish to design his own. Mail them at least two to three weeks before the Court of Honor.

Some Scouts like to include a copy of their Eagle photo with their invitation. Some have the photo copied directly on their invitations.

Ryan Scott Hilbert
Eagle Scout
November 6, 1985

You are cordially invited
to attend the

Eagle Court of Honor

honoring

Ryan Scott Hilbert

November 6, 1985
7:30 p.m.

8217 Deseret Avenue
Fair Oaks, California 95628

Scotty may want to send invitations to his Congressman and State Representative and also to the President. These officials generally respond with a letter of congratulations which is nice to keep in the Eagle scrapbook.

It's also a good idea to send a thank you note with the invitations that are sent to special merit badge counselors and others who have helped the Eagle candidate in some way. A quick and handy way to do this is to use the little paste-on notes that can stick to a surface and then be removed. One Eagle candidate used one of these in each of his invitations where he wanted to include an expression of appreciation. Each note read something like this:

"Thank you for being my Personal Management merit badge counselor. You were a big help on my trek to Eagle!"

Some Scouts whose Eagle projects received newspaper coverage like to include a photocopy of the clipping with the invitation. This lets people know a little more about what the Eagle program is all about. Following are samples of two newspaper clippings:

Gamble's Winner   Boy Scout Mike Gamble did more serving than eating at his March 1 fundraiser for the Statue of Liberty restoration project. Mike sold 150 tickets to his dinner at the Fair Oaks Clubhouse and netted $600. *Photo Courtesy of Fair Oaks Post.*

The Fair Oaks Post

November 9, 1984   Vol. 1, No. 13   10120 Fair Oaks Blvd.   Fair Oaks, California 95628   (916) 965-NEWS   Mailed Circulation: 16,096

On Campus

Scout Sponsors Landscaping For LeGette School

Boy Scout James Speer, of Troop 67 completed his trail to the coveted Eagle rank Oct. 27. The 13-year old Carnegie student worked with 20 other scouts he organized to plant 50 shrubs at Earl LeGette Elementary School along a 500 foot fence.

"The Eagle is suppose to be a project an adult would like to take credit for," said James, who attended LeGette and lives close to the school. "It is a service project that places the scout in a position of leadership. He is responsible to oversee the pro-

ject and co-ordinate other scouts to assist him. This project will help add color and will reduce part of the eyesore the bank creates."

LeGette principal Lynn Montgomery knew James from a previous project. The scout had painted all the kindergarten playground equipment last summer for a merit badge. When James presented his landscaping proposal, Montgomery said he was "very impressed."

"James handled himself in a mature way," the principal said.

"He had the background information and the prices."

James is glad to have met his goal, to have his project completed by November and to be awarded his Eagle before entering high school. His hard work and determination have paid off for him and Earl LeGette School.

The determined scout mowed lawns, recycled newspapers and aluminum cans during the summer and earned $100. The LeGette student council donated money towards the plants as did local Girl Scout Troops 241, 124, and 198. The necessary $257 was raised and the 50 plants purchased.

Scouts usually fund their projects with donations. It is very unusual for the scout to take on the additional responsibility of earning money himself. Ellsworth said, "James is an outstanding scout and boy."

James kept notes on his progress through the project, and said he has learned from the experience. "It takes a lot of planning and preparation," he said, summarizing his efforts over the past six months. "I had some trouble along the way. I learned you can't always rely on your plans. You have to be willing to work around others' schedules."

James Speer raised $257 and recruited fellow scouts to help him beautify the LeGette campus on Kenneth Ave. Photo: Stephen Knudsen

Newspaper story on an Eagle Scout Service Project.

The Program

The actual program is, of course, the most important part of the Eagle Court of Honor. Allow time to coordinate the planning. Two sample programs are included at the end of this chapter. Adapt them to the needs of the Scouts involved.

Local printers will sometimes donate all or part of the printing costs. If this is the case, it would be appropriate to include an acknowledgment on the program along with the names of people who have given other special assistance.

Often the local council service center will be able to supply a special speaker or a slide presentation. The troop or district can also be of assistance with this part of the program.

Many times both County and State government offices will supply resolutions and proclamations honoring Eagle Scouts. Officials from these government offices or their representatives will often be available to present these proclamations at the Eagle Court of Honor. However, be sure to contact them weeks in advance to allow time for scheduling. Designate someone from the troop to contact these offices to see what has been done in the past or to suggest the idea, if the program has never been implemented. (See a sample resolution and proclamation at the end of this chapter.)

Scotty Scout needs to be officially presented at the Court of Honor. Ask the Scoutmaster or an individual close to the Scout to fulfill this special assignment. This person usually tells what the Scout has accomplished, something about his personality, and perhaps some favorite Scouting experiences they have had together.

It's helpful for the Scout or his parents to give this person a brief sheet recapping the Eagle's Scouting and personal achievements. Here's an example of what might be included:

Information Sheet On Scotty Scout
For The Eagle Court of Honor

Scotty Scout has been one of those fortunate young men who has
had the opportunity to participate in many different areas of endeavor.
Since he was a fourth grader he has played the trombone and has developed his talent to the point where he has played in school solo
festivals and has entertained many people. Scotty plays in the high
school jazz band. He also plays in the school symphonic band.

Scotty and his older brother, Sam, have both performed on local
television and in various community benefit shows, playing their in-
struments and singing and dancing.

Scotty is also on the school wrestling team. He likes swimming
and is a good runner. He spends most of his spare time reading mys-
teries and biographies or working on the family computer.

His most exciting experiences in Scouting were learning mountain-
side rappelling and going on a 50-mile hike in the Sierra Nevada.

Scotty has served in a number of leadership positions in his troop
including Troop Musician, Assistant Senior Patrol Leader and Senior
Patrol Leader. He also served as a Den Chief.

He holds a special place in his heart for the two Scoutmasters he
has had, Jim Page and Bill Burdick.

Merit badges to Scotty's credit include the eleven required for Eagle plus Music, Reading, Scholarship, Bugling, Printing, Physical Fitness, Indian Lore, Wilderness Survival, Fingerprinting, and American
Cultures.

Scotty follows the example and dedication of his older brother who
is also an Eagle Scout. His younger brother, Greg, plans to be the
third and last Eagle in the family.

Some parents have prepared a slide presentation of the Eagle showing his baby picture, his Cub scouting days, his sports
or school interests and photos of his Scouting days. This type
of presentation can be humorously narrated. Dads usually do
a good job at this. It adds a special touch to a very special event.

Individualize each Court of Honor to the particular Scout or
Scouts being honored. This makes every one special and enjoyable for all who attend.

As part of the program, some troops like to present a gift
such as the official Eagle Scout neckerchief to the Eagle candidate at the Court of Honor.

The local Scout council may have some special Court of
Honor decorations they are willing to bring to decorate the area

where the Court of Honor is to be held. They often know of entertaining speakers who will recount Scouting experiences of interest to everyone. Someone from the council is often asked to present the actual Eagle certificate. Other times the certificate is presented by a special leader.

It's important to contact everyone participating on the program. Be sure they know what they are to do.

Plan the program well ahead, and everything will usually go according to plan.

A Word of Caution: One Eagle Court of Honor lasted *three hours.* Just about everyone fell asleep (or felt like it). Be sure the planning includes time limits for those who take part. The program will be much more enjoyable if it doesn't last forever.

Refreshments

Plan refreshments well ahead of time. If several Scouts are receiving their Eagle awards at the same Court of Honor the mothers of the Scouts, along with the Scoutmaster, usually do the planning for the food. It's often a matter of seeing who has done this kind of planning in the past and then reviewing all the details with those people. (See checklist at the end of this chapter).

Punch and a cake with an Eagle emblem are always popular. The emblem may be copied from the one appearing on the Eagle napkin or on the front of the Eagle Court of Honor invitation. Anyone skilled in cake decorating will have little difficulty with the design. If a bakery is involved, just give the baker a copy of the design.

Decorations and Displays

Red, white and blue crepe paper will add color to the serving area.

Photos of the Eagle Scout(s) may be used as decorations.

Some troops like to arrange for a display table showing mementos from the Scout's career including his Cub Scouting days, a Scout scrapbook, special awards he may have earned along the way, etc.

The Big Day Arrives

With proper planning, everything will be ready for the big event. All Scouts from the troop should be in full uniform. If possible, the whole troop should be present. Attending an Eagle Court of Honor gives the younger Scouts extra incentive to keep pushing toward this exceptional achievement.

It's wise to go over the checklist one final time. Then everyone can "be prepared" and enjoy the long-awaited day.

Resolution

By Senator John T. Doolittle

RELATIVE TO COMMENDING GREGORY HOCH

WHEREAS, Gregory Hoch of Troop 67 has successfully completed the requirements for the prestigious Eagle Scout Award, the highest award given by the Boy Scouts of America and, in recognition thereof, is deserving of special commendations; and

WHEREAS, Gregory has completed the ranks of Star and Life Scout, and satisfied the requirements for not less than 21 merit badges, of which 11 are in the outdoor, fitness, and service fields, and 10 are in fields of his own choice; and

WHEREAS, Only those young men who have been outstanding in scouting and who have provided exemplary service to their troop and community can receive the Eagle Scout Award; and

WHEREAS, Gregory has developed leadership ability and earned the esteem of his community and his fellow scouts and his scouting achievements reflect the highest ideals of American youth, now, therefore, be it

RESOLVED BY SENATOR JOHN T. DOOLITTLE, That he congratulates Gregory Hoch on his receipt of the Eagle Scout Award, and commend him on his outstanding achievements in qualifying for that high honor; and be it further

RESOLVED, That a suitably prepared copy of this resolution be transmitted to Gregory Hoch.

_____
Senator

_____First_____ Senate District

June 11, 1984

PROCLAMATION HONORING ROBERT HOCH
ON THE OCCASION OF HIS ACHIEVEMENT OF
THE RANK OF EAGLE SCOUT IN
THE BOY SCOUTS OF AMERICA

WHEREAS, ROBERT HOCH is a member of the Boy Scouts of America; and

WHEREAS, ROBBIE has earned the necessary (eleven) merit badges required for the rank of Eagle and has fulfilled other requirements, to include badges for Music, Reading, Scholarship, Bugling, Printing, Basketry, Indian Lore, Wilderness Survival, Fingerprinting, and American Cultures; and

WHEREAS, ROBBIE has demonstrated leadership abilities by serving in a number of leadership positions in his troop and his church, including Assistant Senior Patrol Leader, Troop Musician, and Deacon's Quorum President; and

WHEREAS, ROBBIE has received recognition for his talents in the field of music, with recent performances in two productions of the "Music Circus", on Channel-10's "Moments of Reflection", and in the community production of "Scrooge", as well as performances in various community benefit shows; and has displayed his talents playing the piano at the "Old Governor's Mansion" in Sacramento; and

WHEREAS, ROBBIE's writing skills have earned him several prizes and rare experiences, to include free flying lessons and the opportunity to meet Mrs. Anwar Sadat of Egypt; and

WHEREAS, these accomplishments were instrumental in helping ROBBIE to achieve the rank of Eagle Scout in the Boy Scouts of America; and, in so doing, ROBBIE has followed the example and dedication of his three older brothers in becoming the fourth "Eagle" in his family;

NOW, THEREFORE, BE IT PROCLAIMED that the Sacramento County Board of Supervisors hereby honors ROBERT HOCH for his efforts and accomplishments and especially on his recognition by the Eagle Scout Court of Honor for his achievement of the rank of Eagle Scout in the Boy Scouts of America.

Bill Bryan
SUPERVISOR

ATTEST Beverly G. Williams
CLERK OF THE BOARD

EAGLE COURT OF HONOR CHECKLIST

_____ Schedule a date and reserve the facility

_____ Pick up the Eagle Certificate, papers and Eagle kit at the local council office

_____ Purchase invitations, program covers and napkins
These items are available at the Council Trading Post

_____ Order any plaques or special presentations several weeks before the Court of Honor

_____ Have black and white and color photos taken of the Eagle Scout

_____ Send news release to the local newspaper(s)

_____ Prepare and send Court of Honor invitations

_____ Draft program ideas

_____ Prepare the programs and have them printed

_____ Prepare for flowers or other decorations for the Court of Honor

_____ Plan any Scouting displays to be used

_____ Prepare flowers, tablecloth or other decorations for the serving area

_____ Plan refreshments

_____ _Reminder calls to everyone who is to participate on the program_

Checklist for the Day of the Court of Honor

_____ Check the facility and do the decorating

_____ Have all refreshments and supplies on hand

_____ Make any last minute calls

_____ Be sure uniform is complete

_____ Check microphone and sound system

_____ Set up slide or movie projectors and tape recorders, if these are to be used

_____ Make any last-minute checks regarding the program

_____ Go and have a good time. It's well deserved!

STAR-LIFE
"EAGLE COURT OF HIGH HONOR"
June 27, 19

WELCOME .... David Bassett

POSTING OF COLORS .... Troop 67

INVOCATION .... Matt Smedley

SPEAKER .... Vic Enchelmeyer
District Scout Executive

RECOGNITION AWARD

PRESENTATION OF AWARDS

STAR .... Jerry Amundsen

| Travis Johnson | Troop 67 | Ryan Hilbert | Troop 67 |
| Aaron Gregersen | Troop 67 | Aaron Ewing | Troop 367 |

LIFE .... Jim Gordon

Darin Anderson	Troop 67	Shane Thomson	Troop 54
Craig Crandall	Troop 67	Mike Gamble	Troop 54
Mike Shaw	Troop 67		

PALMS .... Ron Neilson

Todd Ellsworth	Troop 67	Silver	36	merit badges
Tim Karley	Troop 367	Silver	36	merit badges
		Bronze	41	merit badges
Troy Johnson	Troop 67	Bronze	41	merit badges

" EAGLE COURT OF HIGH HONOR"

EAGLES .... Gerry Smith

| Robbie Hoch | Troop 67 | Brett Shirhall | Troop 355 |
| Todd Johnson | Troop 67 | Lance Armstrong | Troop 355 |

SPECIAL PRESENTATIONS

COUNTY PROCLAMATION .... Mr. Tony Russell

SENATE PROCLAMATION .... Senator Doolittle's Administrative Aide

CLOSING

RETREAT OF COLORS .... Troop 54

BENEDICTION .... Justin Jensen

DISMISSAL

Honored Eagle Scouts will leave first to form a reception line in the cultural
hall. All present are invited to offer congratulations.
Refreshments will be served

Todd Johnson
Troop 67

Merit Badges Earned

First Aid
Citizenship in the Community
Citizenship in the World
Citizenship in the Nation
Communications
Environmental Science
Personal Management
Safety
Personal Fitness
Camping Snow
Swimming
Sports
Archery
Astronomy
Lifesaving

Basketry
Bookbinding
Canoeing
Cycling
Dentistry
Leatherwork
Music
Pioneering
Scholarship
Skiing
Reading
Water Skiing
Cooking
Motorboating
Model Design & Building

Todd Johnson

Leadership Positions

Scribe, Patrol Leader, Assistant Patrol Leader, Senior Patrol Leader, Leadership Corps

Recognition

Diving and swimming medals; Outstanding Citizenship Award; Honor Roll; Carnegie Symphonic Band; Community Service to Red Cross Recognition; T.V. appearances and community productions.

Interests

Music, singing, dancing, saxophone, snowskiing, water skiing, swimming, soccer, juggling, stamp collecting and coin collecting. Animals, particularly dolphins and becoming a veterinarian.

Scouting Highlights

90-mile canoe trek; waterskiing and boating super activity; Philmont Scout Ranch; Eagle project; Service at the Special Olympics and being a Scout with my two brothers.

Eagle Project

Transported and dried ll wood-slat benches at our home. The benches were disassembled, sanded, stained, reassembled, and returned to the Folsom Zoo.

Leadership Acknowledgement

Russell Johnson, Dave Smith, Bert Ellsworth, Denny Wagstaff, Tim Chaffin

Eagle Court of Honor Display

Red, white, and blue theme highlights Eagle Court of Honor refreshment table.

10

Flying With The Eagles

Is it all over? Does everything end with the Eagle Court of Honor? No. The exciting fact is that the fun and benefits of earning this prestigious award go on and on. Many of the benefits, in fact, last a lifetime.

Once an Eagle, always an Eagle. In most Courts of Honor, you'll hear the words, "An Eagle Scout is a marked man."

How true this is. The honor carries its own special distinction. The Eagle Scout will always be just that—an Eagle Scout. He'll be recognized wherever he goes as a person who has accomplished something significant. People will look to him to be a cut above everyone else.

An Eagle Scout was once heard saying, "How can you fly with the Eagles when you work with a bunch of turkeys?" A good question. Just because a boy has earned Eagle rank doesn't mean he won't have to work with some turkeys now and again. That's part of life. He just needs to remember who he is and act accordingly. He must continue to be a leader, lifting and helping others whenever he can.

Ah, the look of success on the face of Scotty Scout . . . . . And well deserved.

You're a "Celebrity:" News Releases and Photos

One of the first things that sets the Eagle apart is community recognition. Someone on the Scout Committee is usually appointed to be sure some publicity gets to the local newspapers. If not, the parents of the Eagle can send in a news release and a photo.

A sample news release would look something like this:

FOR IMMEDIATE RELEASE   May 1, 19__
Contact: James Jones, Scoutmaster 233-2111

Scotty Scout Earns Eagle Rank

A Court of Honor will be held Wednesday, June 10, at 7 p.m. in the Fenwick Community Center for Scotty Scout who has earned the prestigious Eagle Scout award. The Eagle is the highest award attainable in the Boy Scouts of America's advancement program.

For his Eagle service project, Scotty sanded and painted the benches and tables at Fenwick Community Park. He supervised 15 Scouts in this two-day work project.

Friends are invited to attend this special Court of Honor.

If two or more Scouts are participating in a Court of Honor, the article in the newspaper and the photos might look something like this:

Scouts Award Eagle Pins To Speer, Johnson

James Speer

Two Fair Oaks youths gained the rank of Eagle Scout at a Troop 67 Court of Honor Aug. 7.

James Speer, 14, and Travis Johnson, 13, earned more than 20 merit badges each in addition to their required community service project to gain scouting's highest award.

Young Speer, a Bella Vista High School freshman, earned 21 badges and planted 50 oleander bushes at Earl LeGette School. Johnson, also a Bella Vista freshman, gained 32 badges and organized a troop project to build and place six benches at Andrew Carnegie School.

Travis Johnson

Some Scouts and leaders like to take their own photographs of the new Eagle. Polaroids work fine. Using a large American flag as a backdrop for the Scout gives a dramatic effect.

Most newspapers require a 4"x5" black and white glossy photo (or larger). Some prefer take their own photographs. As mentioned earlier, some local photographers provide a black and white Eagle publicity photo free of charge.

The person writing the news release should remember the five "W's" and an "H" of journalism—Who . . . What . . . Where . . . When . . . Why . . . and How. Answering these five questions will cover the major points of the Eagle's story and provide most of the news for the article.

Most editors like information on the Eagle Scout project since these projects generally affect the community. Some newspapers like actual photos of the project. This depends on the space available. Larger newspapers have less space to devote and some-times only print an Eagle photo and a caption. Smaller newspapers give the Eagle program more attention.

Eagle Scout Banquets

In addition to newspaper coverage, the council and/or some local service organizations honor Eagle Scouts with a recognition dinner. Community leaders often sponsor Eagles at an annual Eagle Scout banquet. This gives Eagle Scouts an opportunity to receive recognition and meet well-known and successful people in their community.

Philmont Scout Ranch

Some churches and community organizations also sponsor new Eagle Scouts either partially or fully on a trip to Philmont, the national Scout ranch in New Mexico. This can be the experience of a lifetime for a Scout.

Even if this type of travel is not sponsored by local organizations, it may be something every Eagle Scout would want to set as a goal—to sometime be able to spend a week at Philmont. Leaders, also, find this trip a great experience in their Scouting careers.

The National Eagle Scout Association

The new Eagle Scout may want to become a member of the National Eagle Scout Association. This organization provides on-going information on the Eagle program as well as contact with Eagles all over the world.

This is an alumni-type organization for Eagles of all ages. It identifies and mobilizes the many talents and resources of Eagle Scouts everywhere. It is designed to strengthen the Scouting program.

Membership includes a wallet membership card and a subscription to the *Eagletter,* bulletin of the NESA, also a wall certificate suitable for framing (if ordered). Eagles may also join one of the local NESA chapters by contacting the local council service center.

Other Eagle Opportunities and Benefits

New Eagle Scouts often receive letters of commendation from their representatives in Congress and even from the President of the United States.

By contacting his Congressman, a new Eagle may order a flag of the United States which has been flown in his honor over the nation's Capitol in Washington, DC. Various sizes are available.

In most areas, the Sons of the American Revolution include information on their program in with the Scout's approved Eagle papers. This organization promotes an annual essay contest for Eagle Scouts. It encourages new Eagles to write essays on specified subjects dealing with early American history.

Winners are selected at the local, state and national levels. Awards may include dinners, scholarships, and even an expense-paid trip to the nation's capitol or some other designated place in the United States.

* * *

The Boy Scout catalogue features many beautiful plaques, trophies, paperweights, and jewelry to honor the Eagle attainment. These items can serve as gift and recognition ideas, not just at the time of the award, but for years to come.

Last, But Not Least

All through his life, the Eagle Scout will find his achievement to be a benefit. He has learned many skills throughout his Scouting career that will help him and his community. These include basic skills such as outdoor cooking and swimming. They also include critically important skills such as those learned in the First Aid and Lifesaving merit badges.

He has also learned leadership skills and has the ability to communicate with others. He will always be recognized as a leader.

Job Hunting Advantages for the Eagle

It's a distinct advantage for a young man to design a resume or personal data sheet for himself as soon as he has a need to look for work. On this sheet, he can list his Eagle Scout award. A personal data sheet can be made up in several different ways. Here's an example:

Personal Data Sheet

Scott Scout	Birth Date: Dec. 17, 19____
4800 Skyline Drive	Height/Weight: 5'9", 175 lbs.
Anywhere, USA	Physical Condition: Excellent
212-313-3111	Social Security: 565-11-2111

Education: Currently a Senior   - Westwood High School   - 3.8 GPA

Experience:

February to Present   COMMUNITY ANIMAL HOSPITAL   Westwood, FL
Vet assistant and maintenance work - $3.80 per hour. Part time.

Summer, '8__   Northern Pacific Air Cargo   Kodiak, Alaska
Cargo and maintenance work - $7.50 per hour.

19____-19____   LANDMARK SPECIALTIES, INC.   Westwood, FL
Working as needed in my father's business installing computer equipment in offices. $3.50 per hour.

19____-19____   THE CLOTHING STORE   Westwood, FL
Worked part time moving clothing, equipment and shelving. $3.50 per hour - temporary employment.

19____-19____   THE GENERAL STORE   Orangevale, FL
Cash register work, customer service, stocking shelves, inventory, maintenance, sandwich-making and food preparation. $2.50 per hour. Reason for leaving: store sold.

Special Awards and Activities:

Biography & photo published in *Who's Who in American High Schools*	Fall 19____
Eagle Scout Award and Bronze Palm	May, 19____
Fine Arts Fiesta Showcase Award: San Juan Unified School District	19____
Citizenship/Scholarship Awards: Andrew Carnegie School	19____ 19____
Royal Reader Award - Earl LeGette School	19____
Created and sold several puzzles to various national magazines.	19____

References: Joe Wood, Scoutmaster   William Harston, DVM
                  4737 Illinois Ave.   Community Animal Hospital
                  Westwood, FL   6248 Main Ave.
                  967-0919   Westwood, FL
                                           988-1721

When several people apply for the same job, the young man with a sharp resume will stand out. This will be especially true when those important words are part of the information.

The award opens many doors. It's a great way to start a conversation, especially if the prospective employer also happens to be an Eagle Scout. Even if he is not, most people have a good idea of what achieving this rank means, and they are impressed. Many young men have related incidents such as the following:

"Wow. A hundred guys went for the job at the theatre in the mall. I couldn't believe how many were there to apply. The manager said that seeing "Eagle Scout" on my application was the deciding factor. I couldn't believe it. I got the job. Isn't that great?"

When nothing else sets young men apart, the recognition of the Eagle rank will. This is true not just for the local theatre manager but even for the national armed services academies at Colorado Springs, Colorado (the Air Force), West Point, New York (the Army) and Annapolis, Maryland (the Navy).

As an example, Major Daniel E. Hancock, Director of Selections for the Air Force Academy, says, "I received your letter asking if being an Eagle Scout helps someone applying for an appointment to the Academy. Your intuitions are correct. I am an Eagle Scout and a graduate of the Air Force academy. My experience along the Scouting trail toward Eagle truly helped me survive and graduate from the Academy. The ideals embodied in the Scout Oath and Scout Law are very much a part of the Air Force."

He goes on to say, "Being an Eagle Scout is a distinct advantage when applying for the Academy. Eagle Scouts receive a significant number of points in our admission formula. Besides being qualified academically, candidates must be able to perform well outside the classroom. Our statistics show that Eagle Scouts make excellent cadets."

Similar interest in Eagle Scouts was expressed by Major Charles W. Pope, Admissions Media Officer at West Point Military Academy. West Point recognizes the value of Scouting and has a special place on its application form to show "Eagle Achievement."

As noted, this same kind of recognition and respect is true for many other job opportunities, as well, not just in the armed services.

One young college-age man regretted that he never finished his Eagle.

"Now, when I go for a job, I often fill out applications that have a place to mark for completion of the Eagle rank. I have to leave it blank, and I know that puts me at a disadvantage in the job-hunting process."

It's true. The Eagle Scout is definitely a "marked man." At a young age, he's accomplished a great goal, and he and his community can benefit from this attainment for many years to come.

Now What?

Is the Eagle the end of the Scouting trail? Certainly not. Most Eagles like the challenge of the Eagle Palms. For just five additional merit badges, the Eagle can earn a Bronze Palm. For ten, he receives the Gold, and for 15, the Silver. Palms may be worn in any combination to show the number of merit badges earned beyond Eagle.

Palm application forms are available at the local council service center.

A Unit Board of Review must be held for each Palm. An advancement report has to be turned in to the local Scout service center when the Palm and certificate are picked up.

Besides earning Palms, there are countless leadership opportunies for all Eagles. They are always welcome to work with younger Scouts, encouraging them along the trail; they make excellent camp counselors and leaders. Most Eagles also look forward to the day when they can serve as Scoutmasters themselves.

* * *

So, Scotty Scout is an Eagle at last. His opportunities will continue to grow as he exercises his skills and abilities. He, along with Eagle Scouts everywhere, are recognized as leaders and achievers. They are part of a worldwide tradition. They have earned the right to "fly with the Eagles."

Index

A

Advancement, 27, 30
Advancement Committee Member, 48, 107
Air Force Academy, 134
Annapolis, 134
Application, Eagle, 103-108
    Checklist, 109
    Rush Processing, 108
Approval, Eagle Service Project, 81
Armstrong, Neil, 19

B

Baden Powell, Gen. Robert S.S., 21
Banquets, Eagle, 129
Basic Requirements, 37
Benefits of the Eagle rank, 23, 25
Board of Review, Eagle, 105-108
Boy Scout Handbook, 30, 32, 41, 45, 103
  Boy Scout Requirements booklet, 41

C

Calendar, Eagle Project, 75, 77, 88
Camp, Scout, 69-70
Camping, Record of, 71
Catalogue, Boy Scout, 131
Charts:
    Go for the Eagle, 32, 34-35, 41, 45
    Suggested Time Line, 30, 36, 43
    Scouting's Organizational Structure, 57

T

Tenderfoot Rank, 32
Thank You Notes, Eagle Court of Honor, 113
    Eagle Service Project, 86
Three-Legged Stool, 45
Time Line Chart, Suggested, 30, 36, 43
Turkey Scout, 22
Turkeys, Working With, 125

U

U.S. Postal Service, Eagle Papers, 108

W

West Point, 134
Wolf Scout, 21-22
Write-up, Eagle Project, 88-101